D0356809

"At a time when many Christ[...]
sponsibility to house refugees [...]
home countries, *Finding Jesus at the Border* feels like a breath of fresh air. Regardless of your religious beliefs, Julia Lambert Fogg has done all of us a service by asking, 'What would Jesus do?' were he confronted with the inhumanity of our current immigration laws."

—**Reza Aslan**, author of *Zealot: The Life and Times of Jesus of Nazareth*

"A beautifully written, well-researched, painfully moving book that invites all believers to read Scripture in a new way. Reading this book involves pain, hope, and challenge. Any church community that reads it prayerfully will never be the same again!"

—**Justo L. González**, immigrant, church historian, and theologian

"Jesus's exhortation to love one's neighbor as oneself is the simplest and most profound spiritual teaching in human history. His story and teachings dovetail with the journeys of so many of our immigrant neighbors, as Julia Lambert Fogg explores with such compassion in her expert and moving book. Jesus came from a family of immigrants, after all, and as he famously said, 'I was a stranger, and you welcomed me.'"

—**Rainn Wilson**, actor and writer

"This is a moving account of a personal journey into the immigrant world and how it led to a new understanding of Christian faith and Scripture. Fogg creatively interweaves immigrant stories with biblical passages, showing how those experiences can help us read the Bible with fresh eyes. But the goal is not just to inform her readers; she wants to motivate them into action. A challenging read indeed!"

—**M. Daniel Carroll R.**, Wheaton College; author of *The Bible and Borders*

"The issue of immigrant rights, like that of economic justice, requires little translation between the Bible and our time. Vulnerable people who are pushed and pulled by the tidal forces of powerful empires are central subjects of both Testaments. Fogg's work is an engaging addition to the literature that reads Word and world with attention to the displaced and dispossessed who are forced to cross borders."

—**Ched Myers**, coauthor of *Our God Is Undocumented: Biblical Faith and Immigrant Justice*

FINDING JESUS AT THE BORDER

Opening Our Hearts to the Stories
of Our Immigrant Neighbors

Julia Lambert Fogg

BrazosPress

a division of Baker Publishing Group
Grand Rapids, Michigan

Published by Brazos Press
a division of Baker Publishing Group
P.O. Box 6287, Grand Rapids, MI 49516-6287
www.brazospress.com

Printed in the United States of America

Library of Congress Cataloging-in-Publication Data
Names: Fogg, Julia Lambert, 1970– author.
Title: Finding Jesus at the border : opening our hearts to the stories of our immigrant neighbors / Julia Lambert Fogg.
Description: Grand Rapids : Brazos Press, a division of Baker Publishing Group, 2020.
Identifiers: LCCN 2019031835 | ISBN 9781587434303 (paperback)
Subjects: LCSH: Emigration and immigration—Religious aspects—Christianity. | Emigration and immigration—Religious aspects—Christianity—Biblical teaching. | Church work with immigrants—United States. | Church work with immigrants—Mexico.
Classification: LCC BV2695.E4 F64 2020 | DDC 261.8/3—dc23
LC record available at https://lccn.loc.gov/2019031835

ISBN 978-1-58743-464-8 (casebound)

All names and details have been changed to protect the privacy of the individuals involved, with the exception of Hugo Mejia in chap. 5, whose story is in the public record.

20   21   22   23   24   25   26   7   6   5   4   3   2   1

For Sergio
and all the young people
whose dreaming is making these
United States of America
a home for all of us.

Whoever welcomes you welcomes me, and whoever welcomes me welcomes the one who sent me. Whoever welcomes a prophet in the name of a prophet will receive a prophet's reward; and whoever welcomes a righteous person in the name of a righteous person will receive the reward of the righteous; and whoever gives even a cup of cold water to one of these little ones in the name of a disciple—truly I tell you, none of these will lose their reward.

Matthew 10:40–42

Contents

Acknowledgments

Dear reader, I'm so glad you are here. Thank you for coming and listening with open ears. There are so many people who have made your reading possible. I cannot name them all here, but I am grateful to each one for their contributions.

First and foremost I want to thank Marja Mogk. She has read every paragraph of every chapter in this book through almost every iteration I have written over the past five years. And with every (patient) reading, she made the structure more solid, the prose cleaner, and my voice stronger. She has been more than a careful editor and friend; she has tended the very soul of this work. Thank you.

I also want to thank my writing partners from the NCFDD (National Center for Faculty Development and Diversity) boot camp, Maylei Blackwell, Michelle Habell-Pallán, and now Tiffany Willoughby-Herard. Mujeres, has it been four years now? Five? Thank you for all of your advice, grounding, encouragement for self-care, and celebration of every win—great and small—toward the long goal. *Se hace camino al andar.*

Thank you, Messiah-Mesías Lutheran Church, for welcoming me, encouraging me, and teaching me through what were some of the more difficult times in the life of the congregation. You have been a blessing to me.

Thank you to my mentors with CLUE-VC, especially chairs Vanessa Frank, Betty Stapleford, and Nan Waltman. Thank you to Ched Myers for his early feedback and advice on chapters 1 and 2. And a special thank you to the Brazos team of editors, careful readers, and promoters. It is a pleasure to work with all of you.

Thank you to Tatiana, Diego, and Christine, owners and now friends at the cafés where I fueled and refueled, wrote, revised, and re-revised—where would I be without your hospitality, your conversations, and your coffee?

I also want to thank my parents. Mom and Dad, you paved the road for me to do this work by valuing learning, prioritizing education, and giving me opportunities to explore the world. You never said no when I told you about another border I wanted to cross. I know that was scary for you. Thank you for letting me go.

Chris and Sam, Emma, Ian and Jacob, you bring me life and hope. I cannot wait for the world you are shaping to come into full bloom. It is already a world of advocacy and justice that I am impatient to live in now.

Kenneth Paul, you are the music in my life and my partner in the dance. You are my heart, my joy, my home. Thank you for everything.

1

Walk This Way:
Approaching the Border

My Story

I am a fifteenth-generation East Coast American of mixed European and Anglo descent. My ancestors crossed the ocean—and many other barriers, borders, and boundaries going back to the time of William Penn—to come to these shores.[1] But most of those stories of journey and arrival are lost to my generation. We didn't personally cross those borders, and neither did our parents, grandparents, or great-grandparents. Immigrant consciousness disappeared from my family's sense of identity generations ago. Our European ancestors planted their roots firmly in the East Coast soil through deaths and burials, births and baptisms, farming, building, ranching, mining, and yes, serving in political office and as lawyers, educators, engineers, and artists.

Although my own generation was not aware of our immigrant status, I was aware of the presence of more recent arrivals in my hometown. For example, the mushroom workers in

Kennett Square, Pennsylvania, came as immigrant farm workers. As they followed the crops from south to north up the Eastern seaboard, many of these farm workers planted themselves in Pennsylvania soil, settled, and became our neighbors. Others kept moving through the towns around us, following the seasonal work and harvest times. But our new neighbors were invisible to us. We rarely met, and our lives seldom connected. The children of these immigrants weren't in the same public school with me or my brother; their moms didn't shop in the grocery stores we frequented. I had little awareness of national borders, but there were plenty of local borders in the mostly white, semi-rural, suburban regions of southeastern Pennsylvania.

We were more aware of another immigrant group who also farmed for a living, the Pennsylvania Dutch and Amish who lived down the road. We bought fresh corn, string beans, and tomatoes from them. But they weren't new immigrants, and they owned or leased their farmland. Their families had also been in the area for generations. My great-great-grandmother grew from their roots. In middle school, I met some first- and second-generation German, English, Italian, and Irish immigrant children. We all developed the same local American accent, but our names were different. I had no sense of where their families had come from, or which borders their parents had crossed to get here. I do remember that my mother was sad when my friend Tommy's family emigrated to Pakistan. I learned the names of places people left our area *for*, but not the names of the places my friends' parents had come *from*.

Although I grew up regularly going to Sunday school and learning Bible stories on old-school felt boards, I never heard those sacred stories as narratives of border crossing. Instead, what I knew of border crossing came from aunts, uncles, and cousins talking about their time in the Peace Corps or the American Friends Service. I knew their stories, like Tommy's, of crossing borders to live abroad, to teach or to serve, and then to return home.

When it was my turn to go abroad, I found crossing borders to be relatively easy. I studied in Mexico, Nicaragua, and Guatemala. I traveled to Venezuela, Columbia, and Ecuador. I lived in Spain for a few years—I was even, technically speaking, undocumented there for a time. I rarely worried about it. It seemed easy enough to take the train from Madrid to Lisbon (long before country borders dissolved into the European Union), spend the day, and get another short-term tourist visa stamped into my passport on the way back. I never thought twice about returning to the US, as so many international students must today. This was before September 11, 2001. I had an American passport, white skin, and an excellent education. I dressed in a traditionally feminine way, and I was comfortable traveling alone. I rarely drew a second look.

My sense of borders and belonging changed after I moved from the East Coast to California. In Los Angeles, it seemed like everyone I met was a first- or second-generation arrival. In the San Fernando Valley, every other household spoke a different language. Everyone had a unique story of how they arrived, where they came from, and why they wanted or needed to leave where they had been. Living among so many immigrants, I constructed my own story of migration. It went like this: I left home in 2003 and came to California to teach religion in a small, private, liberal arts university. At first, everything smelled different. The desert air was different—lighter, drier, with subtle shades of toasted caramel, creosote, and sage. I missed the thick, heavy atmosphere before a rainstorm in Pennsylvania, electric with lightning and ear-splitting thunder that resolved into clean, clear air after it passed.

Aside from the weather, culture shock hit me in random ways. Southern Californians never stopped smiling. The ocean was on the wrong side. No one knew how to drive in the rain, so the lightest spritz caused accidents. Drivers piled onto "freeways" that stole hours of time from each week. The most baffling cultural shift for an East Coaster, though, was not the language but the dress codes. There weren't any. People wore whatever clothes they wanted to, to any event they attended, and never felt over-, under-, or improperly (as my grandmother would say) dressed. Shorts and flip-flops, or a dress and heels? All were welcome. But the adjustments I made only skimmed the surface of the kinds of cultural and social adjustments people must make when coming from another country altogether.

Encountering Borders inside Southern California

A few years into my teaching career, when the ocean was still on the wrong side, the bishop's office of the Evangelical Lutheran Church in America (ELCA) called and asked if I spoke Spanish. I said yes. Was I also ordained to preside at Communion? I said yes. The bishop's official asked if I was available to preach and preside that Sunday at a Lutheran church in Pasadena. Could I lead two services, one in English and one in Spanish? I actually had never preached in Spanish (except for that one time when I was sixteen and I gave a short, extemporaneous homily, "Dios es amor" ["God is love"], on the border in Mexico during a mission trip), nor had I led a Lutheran liturgy, let alone a Lutheran liturgy in Spanish. I said yes. And with that one phone call, I quickly stepped across three borders—religious, cultural, and liturgical. That Sunday gig turned into five years of part-time bilingual ministry. I fell in love with the immigrant families of the Scandinavian-Latinx congregation I served, and they transformed me.

I write this book to share my experience of crossing borders and the transformations that come when we step out of our comfort zones to meet people, however awkwardly, in their religious, cultural, and linguistic homes.[2] To this end, I set biblical stories of border crossing, migration, and detention in conversation with contemporary stories of border crossing, migration, and detention. This work is personal and theological and, necessarily, political.

During his presidency, Barack Obama increased the deportation of undocumented immigrants who had committed crimes. And in 2012 Obama's administration also provided an avenue for the temporary suspension of deportation procedures for undocumented young people brought to the US as children. This program, Deferred Action for Childhood Arrivals (DACA), stabilized the lives of many youth so that they could work, drive, and normalize their lives. In 2017, Donald Trump's administration attempted to cancel DACA, throwing the lives of almost 700,000 DACA recipients into ambiguity and turmoil.[3] The question of whether the DACA program will continue or be canceled now stands with the Supreme Court.[4]

In 2014, and again in the summer of 2018, tides of children from Latin America flooded the US-Mexico border. Some of the children were as young as six, accompanied by an adolescent or teenage sibling. The children sought one or both parents. Now, under the Trump presidency, Immigration and Customs Enforcement (ICE) agents are working hard to clear the books—that is, to deport as many undocumented immigrants as possible and to clear out overcrowded detention centers and courtroom caseloads that would otherwise be backed up for years to come. President Trump has also canceled protections for Salvadorans, Haitians, and immigrants of other nationalities who have been living legally in the US. When these protections are removed, those who sought and received legal residence in the US after natural disasters destroyed their home economies will find themselves among the undocumented eligible for forced removal. To add insult to injury, the Trump administration is battling child advocates who demand an end to and reparations for the policy of separating children of all ages from their parents at our borders. Most of these families have committed no crimes; they are simply exercising their right under US law to seek asylum at our border. For these reasons, it is increasingly urgent that we hear contemporary stories of immigration, migration, border crossing, and detention in conversation with biblical stories of border crossing.

Working as a Pastor

I learned about this urgency when I was invited to substitute preach at and then to copastor an immigrant church every second or third Sunday over the course of five years. I was part of a small team of part-time, bilingual, and mostly female pastors. To make this arrangement work, the congregation embraced more voluntary lay leadership and self-governance as a way to keep their church open and on its feet until they could afford a full-time pastor. The congregation was small but dedicated. They were also a very culturally complex group of people. The first service was in English, with a beloved Finnish or Norwegian hymn for special occasions, and drew second-, third-, and fourth-generation Scandinavian immigrant families. The second service was in Spanish and drew first-, second-, third-, and fourth-generation members of immigrant Latino families of Peruvian, Mexican, Salvadoran, Guatemalan, Honduran, Nicaraguan, and Chilean descent. Ours was a quintessential immigrant church.

The church held services every Sunday, with occasional baptisms and quinceañeras on Saturdays. A few adults celebrated their First Communion with us. But there was no longer an acolyte program, as there had been a generation ago. Instead, at Sunday services I invited the youngest children up to light the candles and drew their siblings in to collect the offering. They were shy, but excited to participate. We tried to involve everyone in the worship experience. The Lutheran liturgy was beautiful and rhythmic, and it followed a certain informal character—a little bit Latin American and a little bit Scandinavian. The lay worship leaders were an eclectic bunch. Some had graduate degrees from Yale University, others had a fourth-grade education from rural Central American schools. Our pianist was an African American jazz musician who often stayed after Sunday services to give free group piano lessons to the children. The congregational president was a twentysomething bilingual college student whose family was originally from Mexico. Then there was me—the red-headed female professor in a black Presbyterian robe following a Lutheran liturgy. I liked the eclectic mix. Every face reminded us of the four corners of God's earth, gathered together under one roof to sing praises and offer thanksgiving.

The governance of the church followed ELCA protocols, but in worship, denominational boundaries were more fluid. Sometimes I heard private confession from individual church members who had been raised Catholic. They felt they could not receive the Eucharist until they had spoken with me in confession. I adapted house-blessing liturgies for young families who wanted to banish the evil spirits that lurked in their home and frightened their children. I laid healing hands on aching body parts and infections that wouldn't heal; I prayed over deep childhood pains that still festered but were never reported to the authorities. I explained the Trinity—or tried to; I translated intimate conversations between mothers and teenage daughters who didn't speak the same language. As a congregation, we wept with a mother whose son had been deported twenty-four hours after his arrest, and we encouraged each other when members lost their jobs or struggled to feed their children on one income. We listened to grandparents' stories and celebrated parents' hopes and dreams for their American children.

People usually frequented one service or the other according to their language preference and habit. But there were some exceptions. Young people who attended the Spanish service with their parents only understood about half of the liturgy. They were really coming for the cultural connection to their family's heritage. Those who attended the English service came for their friendships and loyalties to the founding families—their parents or grandparents. But occasionally the children's choir would sing at both services, and Angel, a Spanish speaker, would attend the English service to get an early start on his workday. I couldn't help noticing the irony that, even as we proclaimed the one body of Christ on Sunday morning, our two services seemed divided.

Jesus's Stories Merge and Emerge in Our Immigrant Stories

After my own initial leap across the denominational and linguistic borders, the transformations I experienced in the church came more slowly and profoundly. I noticed that my language changed from "your congregation" to "our congregation." I became part of the community, and they became part of me and my thinking and moving in the world. I carried them with me, as my seminary professors had taught me, seeing the world through their questions and perspectives, joys and loves and losses. Then, as I prepared sermons each week for our congregation, I also began to hear the biblical stories I was preaching in new ways. Not all at once, in a single moment of revelation or insight, but slowly. The first thing I noticed was how often Jesus crossed geographical borders to heal people in the Gospels. Then I began to see all the different social boundaries Jesus crossed just to be with people, to eat with them and teach them.

At the same time, the social, linguistic, and cultural borders in our congregation became more obvious to me. The stories of Jesus standing at borders and crossing them stood out against the incongruous—to my thinking—congregational borders people fought to maintain. Before my eyes, the two settings— Jesus in the first-century world, and Jesus in our twenty-first-century, multilingual Southern California world—merged, danced, and mutually revealed insights across the historical distance. I saw parallel stories, the chance meetings of old and new ideas, the exchange of information, shared cultural perspectives, and moments that required repeated translation. All birthed new perspectives. As I swam between the two contexts, the immigrant congregation surrounded my sermon preparation like a cloud of witnesses. On Sunday mornings, I strove to describe the scriptural portals I saw opening up so the congregation could step into the first-century biblical world, walk with Jesus, and return renewed, walking back across that temporal border with ease.

The more I listened, the more the congregational stories echoed biblical stories. I knew Rosa, a woman with mysterious wounds: a fractured hand, a twisted ankle, a swollen knee, a bump on her forehead. The doctors couldn't explain her injuries, just as the experts in Jesus's day could find no reason for another woman's "flow of blood" (Mark 5:25–29). Rosa had been suffering for years, but one morning she caught my elbow and her story poured out of her right there in the sanctuary two minutes before services were to begin. Like the unnamed biblical woman with the flow of blood, Rosa knew the shame and social alienation of a constant, secret pain. Her ailment was not an internal hemorrhage but a husband who abused her. She had borne the abuse, and even "dragged" (his word) her husband to church with her to wash his sins away. On that Sunday, he left her. Rosa arrived at church alone and overwhelmed. Her abuser was gone, but she had no means of supporting herself. She had lost everything. As in the biblical story, there were no physicians with all of the skills needed to address Rosa's ailments; she needed psychiatric attention, legal services, social services, and employment and housing services. Jesus was her only hope. So, she came to the Eucharist, where she reached out and "touched [Jesus's] cloak" (Mark 5:27).

Almost two thousand years ago, long before I experienced this integrating kind of double vision that merged my congregation's stories with Jesus's stories, Matthew wrote his Gospel to merge the ancient saving stories of the Jewish Scriptures with the contemporary, first-century saving stories of Jesus's ministry. The first chapters of Matthew's Gospel open with a reimagining of the exodus: the Jews' suffering oppression and death under a foreign king (Exod. 1:8–14; see Matt. 2:13–15), their subsequent journey out of slavery in Egypt (Exod. 12:37–42; see Matt. 2:15, 19–23), and their wandering in the desert before reaching God's promised land (Exod. 6:1–9).

This was an important story for first-century Jews living under the Roman Empire's oppression. Matthew retells this exodus story through the life of one humble Jewish family (Matt. 1:18–25).[5] Joseph, Mary, and Jesus flee to Egypt seeking refuge from King Herod, who kills a generation of children in and around Bethlehem (Matt. 2:16–18). Herod's "massacre of the innocents" recalls the systematic killing of the Jewish male infants in Egypt as well as God's retribution on Egypt's firstborn (Exod. 1:1–22; 12:12). The child Jesus and his family take refuge in Egypt (Matt. 2:13–15), the home of his Israelite ancestors under Pharaoh (Exod. 1:5–9). Although Matthew doesn't describe Jesus's childhood, the boy lives there until Herod's death, when God calls the family out of Egypt (Matt. 2:19–22; see Exod. 3:7–10). They follow the ancient Israelites' journey north, eventually settling in Galilee. By interweaving the two narrative arcs—Jesus's migration with his family and the Israelite migration out of Egypt—Matthew shows that Jesus represents more than one individual's story (Matt. 2:15).[6] After Jesus makes the rough journey south to escape oppression and death threats from one king, he also goes north, crossing the same borders his ancestors did when they left the violence, slavery, and oppression of Egypt.

The narrative arc Matthew develops (flight from Bethlehem under Herod recalls flight from Egypt under Pharaoh) continues today. Families are fleeing Salvadoran towns run by the MS-13. Others have fled Tijuana, which is run by the Sinaloa cartel. And families will continue to flee unsafe, oppressive situations to find safety and opportunity for themselves and their children. Setting out on a journey to find another place to raise a family and earn a living is the same arc many in our congregation followed. I saw parallels to Jesus's childhood in the lives of the undocumented teenagers and middle-schoolers in our congregation, children who didn't belong to the US or to Mexico. Some young parishioners got into trouble with the law, like Moses (Exod. 2:11–15), and fled, leaving their parents behind. Listening to congregants' stories in tandem with Matthew's reimagined exodus story, I understood the life of Jesus in new ways. I saw whole passages of Scripture differently when I set them side by side with the experiences of people in our congregation. I found that Jesus's life encompassed, echoed, and dignified the congregation's own stories. The more I prepared my sermons with and for these American immigrants of multiple generations, the more clearly I saw the deep connections between the ancient biblical narratives and the contemporary, lived experiences of God's people in Southern California.

Why Should We Listen to the Stories of Undocumented Migrants?

The Bible is and has been an important resource for immigrants, migrants, and border crossers. The general secretary of the World Council of Churches once called the Bible "the ultimate immigration handbook,"[7] and the name has stuck. When we read Scripture as an immigration handbook, we hear the stories differently. This means we can't sit back in our home pews or classrooms or recline in our climate-controlled offices and expect the Scriptures to open up and sing for us. The Scriptures will not begin conversing with our present-day contexts without our engaged effort. Interpretation takes work. It requires us to be present at the borders of time, culture, and circumstances. It requires stepping out of our own neighborhoods and out of our own comfort zones. It requires engaging our neighbors at a deeper level so that we can hear and open our hearts to their stories.

This book argues that to hear the border narratives in our Scriptures we must listen to the stories of those who cross borders and those who live at the border of belonging: the immigrants, the undocumented, the asylum seekers, children separated from their families.[8] With this book I invite you to make that effort. I invite you to really listen to your neighbors' stories, to wrestle with their experiences as undocumented people, and to imagine what it's like to walk in their shoes, navigating the public school system, the emergency room, a courtroom, or an insurance claims office. I invite you to ask what it's like seeking help from a local congregation instead of giving it, receiving charity rather than making an offering, figuring out the tax system, seeking worker's disability, or understanding tenant rights. Transformation begins here: listening to our neighbors' stories. Along the way we will meet neighbors we may not have even known we had.

A few things are important to establish before we begin. This book does not seek to illuminate the complicated nexus of immigration law and policy in the US. I am not a lawyer, policy writer, or even an immigration expert. This book is about us as Americans, as compassionate people of faith who are committed to Jesus's command to "love your neighbor as yourself" (Matt. 22:39). Each chapter offers a deep reading of a Gospel narrative or Pauline letter[9] in conversation with the narratives of specific people who have immigrated to California. I have chosen the stories of these families because they are the people I know, and their testimonies have challenged and changed me. I have also chosen these stories because they are both unique and representative of what many immigrants experience. Most of the people whose voices I lift up here are the parishioners and neighbors with whom I have celebrated, worshiped, and prayed. We have shared in memorial services, court hearings, baptisms, quinceañeras, ESL classes, Bible studies, graduation celebrations, marriages, First Communions, "know your rights" workshops, weekly meals, and youth programs. In short, we have been Christians side by side. In the final chapters, I also lift up the voices and experiences of people whom I don't know well, and of one whom I haven't met in person. This book is one way to begin fulfilling my commitment to them all—to share their stories and lift up their voices across the borders we Americans construct out of our cultures, races, ethnicities, languages, politics, and social classes. This work is a lived theological commitment briefly explored in a series of biblical studies. I believe that listening to ancient border crossers and contemporary border crossers reveals God at work in peoples' lives in exciting and transformative ways.

The aim of this book is to help readers understand the experience of migration and border crossing through the eyes of the people crossing those borders. Crossing borders is not just something Jesus did—it is something all people of faith are called to do. We must cultivate and deepen our empathy for the person who, like Jesus, "has nowhere to lay [their] head" (Matt. 8:20). From here it can be a short step to following Christ alongside and even across new borders—whether physical, emotional, ethnic, racial, political, social, or geographical. When we practice intentionally crossing borders to follow in Jesus's footsteps, we strengthen our Christian vocation and deepen our commitment to serve the body of Christ incarnate in this world. When we listen to brothers and sisters in Christ tell their stories of crossing borders to seek asylum, to find economic opportunity, or to pursue the American dream, we hear Jesus's voice embodied now in their experiences.

What Can We Do? What Must We Do?

The flood of child immigrants from Central America and Mexico—coming with and without parents—increased and reached a crisis point in the summer of 2018. The situation is, however, far from resolved today. How the church responds will depend on three things:

1. A broad exploration of the Scriptures that speak of border crossing, offering shelter, and loving our neighbors
2. An extended encounter with undocumented individuals and mixed-status families whose lives are forever changed by border crossing
3. A growing theological understanding that crossing borders is part of our call as Christians because we follow the incarnate Word, who crossed the greatest border of all—that between the Creator and the created—to walk with us

Addressing the problem of our indifferent Christian responses to the plight of immigrants within our borders and those arriving at our borders is an opportunity for renewing our churches and deepening our discipleship. On the one hand, mainline congregations in the US are suffering deep existential anxiety as their membership numbers diminish. On the other hand, evangelical congregations have been losing members much more slowly. This means that evangelicals have more influence relative to Protestants and Catholics.[10]

In the midst of these demographic trends, many Christians and Christian groups are in a process of transformation.[11] Congregations who, out of fear of one kind or another, are circling their wagons around shared identities—homogenizing into their own ethnic, political, linguistic, or social class enclaves—will be left behind. The paths toward a future church in America lie across and outside our self-imposed and fear-driven "borders."

For example, many churches, like the Lutheran churches I have served in Southern California, were built by immigrants fifty or one hundred or more years ago. But today these gorgeous church buildings—campuses, really—are almost empty. The elders, members of sessions, and councils are in their seventies and eighties, exhausted and crushed by the sense that their generation has failed to keep the church going. They see very little hope in revitalizing their congregations, whether because the demographics of the neighborhood have shifted around them, or because all of their children and grandchildren are, of necessity, more mobile. They leave for school, jobs, or quality of life opportunities elsewhere (just as our neighbors south of the border are doing). What was originally a church established by Scandinavian immigrants to centralize their social lives and support their cultural heritage has become a space the next generations can no longer maintain. What we have not seen, what we must develop the eyes to see, are the new waves of immigrants living our grandparents' dream all around us in the vibrant working-class immigrant families in our neighborhoods. Understanding immigration and the immigrant experience is critical to the life of US churches.

Congregations have a chance to engage the world when they reread Scripture through an experiential hermeneutic of border crossing. This hermeneutic opens us to the voices of our immigrant and undocumented neighbors. Such voices of courage can kick-start our imaginations and draw us out of ourselves to follow a border-crossing Christ. Through careful biblical exegesis, this project explores the ways in which the lives of believers are intertwined with the experience of both biblical and contemporary border crossing. Whether it is standing on the streets in Washington, DC, or walking the strawberry fields in Oxnard, California, Christ calls us to live in the borderlands of church and sidewalk; of country and nation; of belief and secularism; of Catholicism, Protestantism, and evangelicalism; of first-, second-, and third-generation Americans; and in the invisible borderlands of neighbors sharing the same city streets. Living in these borderlands and learning to cross these borders as a regular ethical and spiritual practice of faith will recommit our congregations to the deep social, political, and economic need for social justice in our school systems and our communities. Such ministry to immigrants who have—like Christ and with Christ—crossed borders revitalizes, reconfigures, and may even save our congregational life and outreach.

Fleeing without Papers

Matthew 2:1–23

Santiago's Story

Santiago[1] came across the border from Mexico almost thirty-three years ago, a baby in his mother's arms. Her name is Maria. At that time she was fleeing poverty and the violence of an abusive marriage to seek a better life for herself and for her son. Once she reached California, she settled in an immigrant Mexican community. She remarried. She had another son. She lost her second husband—a US citizen—to military service abroad in Iraq. She moved again. Her boys grew up speaking primarily English and some Spanish with an American accent. They went to public school, played soccer, attended church, and got fairly good grades. There were gangs in the area, but Santiago managed to keep himself and his little brother out of trouble.

Many teenagers experience a rough time when they transition from middle school to high school. They have to negotiate rapidly developing social identities and biological changes. At the same time, these young people are exposed to increasing violence, an overwhelming social media presence, and sexual pressures. Many are socially, psychologically, or financially vulnerable to joining gangs, taking drugs, getting pregnant, or quitting school. Santiago made it through that gauntlet.[2]

If you ask him, he will tell you the church "saved" him. A local Lutheran church offered after-school activities and, most importantly, the church pastor committed to giving Santiago and his friends a ride from school to the church. That pastor's commitment and strong adult mentoring kept Santiago away from the gangs that also recruited for their after-school "activities."[3] Santiago's choice of church over gangs kept him safe.

Then everything ground to a halt around Santiago's fifteenth birthday. He found out he was different from the other kids. He had no legal documents, no birth certificate, no Social Security number, and therefore no legal identity. Because he was undocumented—an "illegal alien" according to the law—he didn't belong. Everything he had always taken for granted— life in California, his friends, his education, his family, even being American—fell away. If he wasn't American like all the other kids, what was he? Who was he? He didn't feel Mexican—he had no memory of Mexico or his Mexican father. His mother had no photos of their relatives or her home in Mexico. He had no Mexican birth certificate. In grade school, Santiago had studied the US government as "our" government. He had learned US history as "our" history, "our" democratic experiment, and "our" land of opportunity—but this American identity was no longer his. He was not part of "us," and—this was the ultimate betrayal—he never had been. It was all a lie. He felt as if he had been torn out of the womb that had nurtured him for the last fourteen years. Why didn't America want him?

Santiago's grades crashed. He withdrew from his friends, his church, even his brother, Omar. Omar, three years younger than Santiago, is officially American. Omar had a California birth certificate and baby photos with his American father. Somehow, Omar belonged. Santiago had no one to talk to about his discovery. His mother didn't understand much English, let alone the future implications of his legal status. Omar had no idea his older brother had been born in a different country or that they had different legal rights in the US. Santiago was terrified someone would discover his secret. He felt alone, isolated, invisible in plain sight. Could he trust the college counselors at school? It was easier to avoid them. Career counselors? What could they do for him? His only work option was cash under the table as a dishwasher or gardener. Lawyers? He was a teenager—how could he pay legal fees? He couldn't focus at school. He stayed home or sat in detention for acting out. He failed that year and attended summer remedial classes. The school held him back a grade anyway. He was a ghost, drifting through his life because none of it was truly his.

Santiago's existential crisis was compounded by the intense anxiety he felt for his mother, Maria. She too was undocumented. What if she were arrested and sent back to Mexico? How could he and his brother survive? What if the police came and took him too? Who would feed his brother, pay the rent, buy school supplies and clothes? How would he survive in Mexico? It was too much to think about. Depression took over. Santiago barely graduated high school.[4]

Families Crossing Borders: God's People

Santiago's story is not unique. In the history of God's people, the flight of refugees recurs across the centuries and echoes through the biblical narrative. In every generation, under different empires, God's people were on the move. In times of political turmoil, famine, and economic hardship, individuals, families, and tribes in the ancient Near East—today's Middle East—sought shelter or grazing lands in Egypt, and, when circumstances changed, they moved north and east, away from Egypt. In this way, following the same migratory patterns, many Jews settled throughout northern Africa, especially Egypt, along the Mediterranean coast, through the Arabian Peninsula, and across adjacent lands. They followed these patterns both before and after the exodus, when Moses led his people out of slavery and into the wilderness, en route to a promised land.[5]

It is in this context of historical Jewish migrations and life as a religious-ethnic minority under foreign empires that Matthew, a Jew, opens his Gospel with a genealogy. Matthew's genealogy is a roll call of Jesus's ancestors who put their faith in God and migrated when they were called to migrate. Thus begins the story of one first-century child born under the Roman Empire and carried across borders in his mother's arms.

From Judea to Egypt and Back

Like Santiago, Jesus was very young when his family crossed the geographical borders of Roman Palestine, also known as Judea, and traveled south into Egypt to escape political violence in his hometown, Bethlehem, the city of the most renowned Jewish king, David. Matthew tells the story this way:[6]

> Now after [the wise men] had left, an angel of the Lord appeared to Joseph in a dream and said, "Get up, take the child and his mother, and flee to Egypt, and remain there until I tell you; for Herod is about to search for the child, to destroy him." Then Joseph got up, took the child and his mother by night, and went to Egypt, and remained there until the death of Herod. (Matt. 2:13–15)

Matthew's story of Jesus's birth bears a striking resemblance to stories of immigrant children carried across borders in their mothers' arms today. Consider the choices the holy family had to make before the boy Jesus was even weaned. When Joseph hears of the political threats against his child (Matt. 2:13), he must decide whether to flee with his family or to send Mary and the baby away. Perhaps he should stay in Bethlehem, work, and send money back when he can. But can Mary and the child make a journey to safety alone? The roads are dangerous, and it's best to travel in large groups. Still, a traveling group can sometimes turn on you or take advantage of you while you sleep. You never know whom to trust, where to rest, what to eat. If the family makes it to Alexandria—a journey that could take weeks—they may be able to locate some distant relative in a nearby village. But these are all guesses; nothing is certain except the voice of God telling them to flee. According to Matthew, the danger to their son is real, imminent, and terrifying. They must leave quickly.

Consider Mary's prospects as a refugee in Egypt. As a new wife and mother, she leaves her home, her sisters, cousins, aunts, and neighbors—all of the more experienced women who could support her and help her raise her first child. Couldn't she just go into hiding among them? But what if King Herod's violence spreads beyond Bethlehem? Herod the Great could be erratic and vicious when he felt threatened. But fleeing all the way to Egypt? Wasn't Joseph strong and able to provide for his family by working with his hands? Perhaps Mary's family had a few resources beyond their own labor. Matthew writes that with the coming slaughter, the holy family must choose now: follow the divine dreams, flee south, and save their boy, or remain where they are and hide from the coming violence. According to Matthew, they follow the divine command and flee.

The holy family travels south from Bethlehem in the province of Judea, through Idumea, across the province of Arabia Petraea, all the way to Egypt. While some immigrant children, like Santiago,[7] never know their father, Jesus's earthly father, Joseph, was with him from the start. Joseph cannot hide his small family from Herod's death squads, but with God's help they can escape. He obeys the divine imperative to take "the child and his mother by night" (Matt. 2:14). He loads everything they have on a donkey, or perhaps on his own back, and leads them south. The walk takes about a month. They cover roughly five hundred miles, traveling across multiple borders between the kingdoms under Rome's imperial rule.[8] God leads Joseph and guides him in dreams, watching over the holy family. Matthew doesn't tell us where they shelter on the way, with whom they stay once they arrive, where they settle, or how long they remain in Egypt.

Matthew Interweaves Migrant Stories[9]

In fact, Matthew has not invented an Egyptian escape route for Jesus and his family at all. Following biblical history, Matthew weaves the fibers and threads of Israel's migrations into Jesus's birth narrative. This is Matthew's interpretive strategy. The interwoven threads create a deep connection between the history and story of God's covenant people and the experiences of God's incarnate Son. Matthew shows that Jesus walks the same migrant path of God's people in order to fulfill Israel's story.[10]

In addition to weaving Jesus's beginnings from the threads and patterns of Israel's beginnings, Matthew's interpretive strategy also affirms that God is faithful to the immigrants, the border crossers, and the ones fleeing oppressive political and economic situations. God rescued the people from their oppression in Egypt, and God rescues the holy family from a local king in Judea. God sustained God's people wandering in the desert, and God sustains the holy family, leading them out of their life as refugees in Egypt. According to Matthew, this fulfills God's own words in Hosea 11:1: "Out of Egypt I called my son" (Matt. 2:15). Hosea recounts Israel's journey out of Egypt using family language. The prophet imagines God's whole people as "a child" suffering and preparing to cross the desert, like so many immigrant children coming to the US today. According to Hosea, God claims the immigrant child, Israel, as God's son, frees the child from violence and oppression, and leads the child across desert borders to establish a new home. Matthew borrows Hosea's prophecy, written after the exodus, and applies the family language to Jesus almost eight hundred years after Hosea's prophetic words. While "my son" refers to Israel in Hosea, Matthew applies "my son" to the young refugee Jesus, traveling with his parents.[11] By weaving the narrative trajectory of exodus and the prophetic words of Hosea into the birth narrative of Jesus, God once again calls a family out of Egypt. This family is seeking a promised land of safety for their son, carrying all of the hopes, fears, and expectations of those who, Matthew affirms, are the people of God.

Additional threads in Matthew's Gospel connect Jesus to Moses, a key figure in the exodus.[12] This connection further strengthens Matthew's interweaving of the exodus with Jesus's migration story in Matthew 2.[13] In Egypt, God's people suffer forced labor, food insecurity, and a kind of ethnic cleansing ordered by Pharaoh's command: kill all the male Jews at birth or, failing that, drown them in the Nile (Exod. 1:11–16, 22; 3:7). Matthew's story of "the massacre of the innocents" mirrors Pharaoh's killing of children and provides the impetus for Jesus's family to flee Bethlehem: "When Herod saw that he had been tricked by the wise men, he was infuriated, and he sent and killed all the children in and around Bethlehem who were two years old or under" (Matt. 2:16). Jesus, like Moses, barely escaped the command of a local ruler to kill children. Unfortunately, this kind of massacre is also well known in Latin America. Dictators have murdered children, whose deaths are revealed to the public only when the cries of groups like the Mothers of the Disappeared rise up like Rachel's weeping at Ramah (Matt. 2:18).[14]

It is likely that Matthew and his community knew of another parallel between the Israelites' treatment under Pharaoh and the Jews' treatment under Herod. The suffering of God's people under forced labor characterized both the Israelites' life in Egypt and the experience of first-century Jews conscripted into Herod's building program.[15] Exodus describes the harshness of the labor conditions under which Pharaoh's slaves worked (Exod. 1:13–14). When they complained, their rations were cut, their work intensified, and supplies for completing the work were withheld (5:4–19). Although Matthew is writing at least seventy or eighty years after Herod the Great's rule, Herod's building program was still famous throughout the Roman Empire. Herod was particularly renowned for expansion and enhancements of the Jerusalem temple.[16]

The unequal power relationship in labor, construction, and agriculture continues today. In California, immigrant agricultural workers have few protections under the law if they are undocumented. And they are uninformed of the rights they do have, so they are afraid to speak out. The agricultural workers who *are* documented also suffer abuses in the fields because they too desperately need the seasonal, skilled, and physically demanding work. To challenge or protest unsafe work conditions under contemporary US labor laws might jeopardize their jobs.[17] Women and girls face sexual abuse and isolation as well as harm to their unborn children through exposure to pesticides.[18] The language barrier for immigrant agricultural workers often means that the indigenous people from Mexico and Central America are treated poorly because they don't speak Spanish or English.[19]

A final narrative parallel Matthew weaves from the exodus story into Jesus's birth story is the conflict between God and local kings over who is to be sole ruler of the Jewish people. In Exodus, Pharaoh and God battle for control of the Hebrew slaves, but God finally wins possession of them after destroying Egyptian crops, water supplies, fields, herds, and armies.

Matthew's readers may hear this battle between Pharaoh and God in the Jewish Scriptures echoed in the power struggle between King Herod the Great and a baby born "king of the Jews." At the very least, Herod feels threatened, just as did Pharaoh. "Wise men from the East came to Jerusalem, asking, 'Where is the child who has been born king of the Jews? For we observed his star at its rising, and have come to pay him homage.' When King Herod heard this, he was frightened, and all Jerusalem with him" (Matt. 2:1–3; compare Exod. 1:8–10).

In Matthew's scene, Herod "and all Jerusalem with him" interpret the wise men's proclamation as pointing to the birth of another king. But Herod will not stand for rivals.[20] He had no problem having his family members, even his own sons, assassinated. Ancients joked that it was safer to be a pig in Herod's house—since Herod wanted to show the Jews that he kept a kosher diet—than it was to be a son, who might challenge his father for the throne.[21] When Herod learns of one "born king of the Jews," he reacts by killing children to destroy any competition to his throne. Herod's edict mirrors Pharaoh's command to kill all boys as they are born to Hebrew women in order to prevent a slave uprising (Exod. 1:10). Both Pharaoh and Herod see their rule threatened by Jewish children who might free their Jewish workforce.

Matthew references another kingly rivalry by identifying Jesus's birthplace as Bethlehem (Matt. 2:2, 5). Like the paradigmatic King David, Jesus is born in Bethlehem and given the title of king at a young age (Matt. 2:1–6). As a young man, David famously rivals King Saul for the throne. Because God is with David, King Saul is afraid and tries to have David killed on the battlefield. Saul even picks up a spear to kill David with his own hands (1 Sam. 18:9–12, 28–29; 19:10–17). David flees Saul's presence multiple times, in fear for his life (e.g., 19:2,

11–13; 20:42). Although the circumstances are different, David and Jesus are fleeing from kings who fear their very presence among God's people. Matthew introduces Jesus in the opening verse of the gospel as "son of David" (Matt. 1:1). With this title, their shared birthplace, and their rivalry with the current king, Matthew sets up two expectations: Jesus, like David, is greater than the man currently on the throne, and, tragically, there will be more conflict and violence to come.

Children, Rulers, and Immigrant Families Today

Today, all across Mexico and Central America, mafia kingpins, drug lords, and corrupt local leaders continue to threaten children and their families. The warning comes not in a dream, as it did for Joseph, but in a note left in a lunch bag or through a dead pet on the doorstep, or in a threat to rape a sister if her brother refuses to carry drugs for the local gang. In Latin America, families are pressured by such "kings" who kidnap, terrorize, and lure children into life-threatening acts. Each family must decide how to respond—but it's an impossible choice. Do we all flee? Do we send our teenage boy north to safety by himself? Do we send our daughter to live with her cousins in Kansas? How will she get there? Where can we all go with so few resources? Which child do we save, and whom do we leave behind?

Even after children or families flee, there are more dangers en route to the US border. Journalist Sonia Nazario interviewed and followed children who rode the trains out of Central America, risking life and limb to escape to the north.[22] She also documented their lives once they arrived at the border. She wrote of children who developed addictions to sniffing glue in order to escape the suffering and poverty they experienced at the border. More recently, there are the heart-wrenching interviews with children under five who have been separated from their parents at the US border and put into temporary shelters. There are the images of children traveling north in caravans from Central America to escape violence, hunger, and poverty.[23] Like Pharaoh or Herod the Great in their time, US leaders today are calling these children a threat to US national security, economic stability, and the American way of life.

The stories of the children fleeing to and living at the Southern California border are not precise parallels to Jesus's flight, but they do illuminate his story in critical ways. The resonances between them invite us to imagine the broader situation of the holy family's first-century dilemmas through the circumstances of the immigrant and refugee families living all around us. And these resonances remind us that the caravans of children fleeing north today are also beloved of God. This mode of reading contemporary immigrant stories alongside Jesus's story of migration follows Matthew's interpretive strategy of reading Jesus's birth story and migrations in relation to the exodus story and the migrations of the Jewish people.

Indeed, the scriptural trajectory—out of peril into safety, out of oppression into promise—does not end when we close our Bibles. God continues to call us today. Hearing Matthew's interpretive reading of the exodus interwoven with Jesus's birth, and then extending this story of God's people to today, we can glimpse God shaping the dreams of fathers seeking to save their sons, mothers seeking to give their daughters opportunities, and families striving to stay alive by migrating out of the oppression, violence, and death that surrounds them. Following the geographical trajectory of Scripture, one can see God continuing to appear at the political borders of today's nation-states, calling, leading, encouraging, and *freeing* God's people. The question for US churches is this: Are these children, whether accompanied or migrating alone across the border, not also the sons and daughters of God? Are they not making their own exodus out of economic oppression or ethnic violence in Mexico, Nicaragua,

Honduras, or Guatemala and seeking a "promised land" in the US as so many other American immigrants have done?

Contemporary Immigration Stories Illuminate Scripture

Just as Matthew's strategy of interweaving our biblical ancestors' stories helps us understand the gospel more deeply, so too do the stories of Santiago, Maria, Omar, and others today. Interwoven stories root the listener in the common story that our faith ancestors lived, reflected on, and recounted to the next generations. When Christians today retell the biblical stories side by side with our own stories of border crossing, and when we share the stories of immigrants now living among us, we can use Matthew's strategy. By interweaving contemporary immigrant narratives with those of Scripture, we bind ourselves as brothers and sisters to those who are on a journey, and we root ourselves more deeply in common identity with the baby carried across the border and through the desert. For Matthew, one cannot understand Jesus without Israel or, indeed, Israel without Jesus. Woven together, the whole cloth illuminates both stories.

Today's churches seeking to understand the stories of immigrant families and children crossing borders can use Matthew's strategy. By listening compassionately to contemporary immigration stories, we more fully understand Matthew's story of Jesus as a child migrant. And reading Jesus's story alongside the stories of refugees and children crossing borders today, we can better understand who they are as God's people. It is by reading the whole cloth—Jesus's story in ours and our stories in Jesus's—that we begin to understand ourselves in relation to the greater scriptural narrative of border crossers.

Just as God appears in the lives of our migrant biblical ancestors and in the stories of the many refugee families now seeking safety at our physical borders, God also appears on the *political* borders of today's nation-states—leading, encouraging, calling, and freeing people for service to God. When we meet DREAM-ers[24] in the US, might we not also be meeting Jesus in our neighbor? In our encounters with young border crossers, might God be seeking to transform us—we who wish to think of ourselves as the people of God? And as we are being transformed, may we be empowered to also step beyond stereotypes to begin walking in solidarity with our immigrant neighbors.

Jesus's Story Continues: Interweaving Immigrant Stories

The road home, like the exodus, is not a straight path for any immigrant family, and it probably was not for the holy family. Although Jerusalem cools politically after Herod's death, Matthew mentions that Joseph, Mary, and Jesus still cannot return to Bethlehem. After crossing the Arabian Peninsula and the Gaza strip, they avoid Bethlehem (Matt. 2:22), continuing north, finally settling down in a village called Nazareth in the Roman province of Galilee (2:23). The holy family may have been among economic refugees as well as political dissidents, runaway slaves, and people hiding from the law who also made their homes in Galilee.[25]

Matthew leaves the family's situation in Galilee open to imaginative reconstruction. Perhaps Matthew's audience knew Galilee well enough that they could fill in the details. In any case, learning more about undocumented children in the US helps us to imagine some of the first-century difficulties. Santiago grew up in the US speaking his mother's Spanish with an American accent; Jesus may have spoken his parents' language, Aramaic, but with an Egyptian accent. Perhaps both boys' clothes would have looked slightly strange to the other local boys they played with on the street. Jesus's shirt may have come as a hand-me-down from fellow Jews in Egypt; Santiago's first sneakers may have come from the refugee bins at the border. It could be that Matthew's Jesus grew up alongside other immigrants and refugees in a Jewish neighborhood in Alexandria, speaking Aramaic at home but learning Coptic or Greek in the marketplace, at school, or playing in the sandy streets. He may have been educationally illiterate, as most ancients had little formal training in reading and writing.[26] Or Jesus may have studied the Jewish scriptures in Greek or Hebrew in the local synagogue with an Alexandrian rabbi; perhaps Jesus even adopted the rabbi's accent. Almost surely, Matthew's Jesus was functionally multilingual and adept at code-switching,[27] regularly moving between linguistic borders.

Santiago's story and Jesus's story in Matthew intertwine and illuminate parallel human experiences. God calls people to cross borders. God accompanies God's people out of situations of violence and abuse, economic slavery, political oppression, and personal degradation. When people obey God's call to cross borders and seek shelter for their families, the road is not easy or quick or safe. The journey does not immediately solve everything. Sometimes it takes generations, as it did in the exodus wilderness, for God to shape and transform and nurture a people. But in the biblical narratives, when individuals respond with obedience, God saves them from slavery, violence, and oppression. Matthew shows that the same God who led people across a border as a pillar of fire and smoke (Exod. 13:21–22) repeated that border crossing out of Egypt. It is not so far-fetched today to consider that God has also called teenagers from Central America and Mexico to make their way north across desert wilderness to reveal God's salvation in a promised land called "America." Perhaps from God's call to Latin American children we can learn a deeper understanding of God's command to "love your neighbor as yourself" (Matt. 22:39).

Santiago's Story Continues: Growing Up and Contributing

When I began preaching at Santiago's church, he was taking classes at a community college. I did not know that he was also, quietly and hardly daring to believe it would be possible, inquiring about enrolling in a four-year university. He was admitted. Funding was found, gifted, and provided bit by bit. He had been the first in his family to finish high school and now he would be the first to graduate from college. At the same time Santiago was enrolling to complete his BA, the congregation that had raised him was shrinking and struggling. The church was unable to officially hire anyone as summer staff, and there were no youth directors. There was no money at the church for that level of programming. But there was, of course, a need. Santiago and I created the first quinceañera program for the church. This program aimed at getting Latina girls to college by building their leadership skills and directing their passions toward community service.

Santiago ran the workshops on college applications, essay writing, and tutoring. He organized fundraisers for college supplies. He became a community activist and educator, informing families in his neighborhood about their rights and available resources. He ran workshops at community colleges about DACA (Deferred Action for Childhood Arrivals), DAPA (Deferred Action for Parents of Americans), and AB540 (California Assembly Bill 540, which allows a tuition exemption for nonresident students attending California public universities).[28] As part of the quinceañera formation and preparation at our church, we invited the birthday girl, her family, and her friends to visit colleges. We all piled into a van and drove to local college campuses to speak with admissions officers and hear about the possibility of attending a four-year college either with or without US citizenship. I wrote the quinceañera liturgy and counseled the girls, their parents, sisters, cousins, and any friends who accompanied them. They learned more than their dance routines. They practiced public speaking in front of the congregation, took notes during sermons, and researched a contemporary issue to teach to the other kids.

Latino families came to us for their *quince* celebrations because we didn't charge them to use the sanctuary or to attend
the college-visit program. All were welcome. It was enough
that they discovered a church interested in educating their children and also providing resources for college. It was enough
that the families began to understand the power of their social
networking as they raised money for their quinceañera celebrations. This networking skill, Santiago argued, was also how
they could work together to raise the money for college. They
learned about California's AB540 law and then studied together
to understand the benefits and limits of DACA.

Working with generations of immigrants in this way, walking
with them as they deepened their faith, raised their children,
and negotiated an educational system that few were familiar
with, required me to have flexibility and an open mind. The
young people and their families insisted on Spanish-language
services for their quinceañera celebrations, baptisms, and weddings. Although few of the kids or young people spoke much
Spanish at all, Spanish was how they connected to their family heritage and culture, just as the Norwegians, Finns, and
Germans had proudly maintained their language, culture, and
heritage through church liturgies and songs. Santiago was an
indispensable guide, and together we figured out the best programming for our community's needs. He knew what worked
in his community and what was most valued. He accompanied
me on regular pastoral home visits. Even though I was only
serving as Sunday morning pulpit supply, pastoral presence in
the congregants' homes mattered deeply. Santiago made sure it
happened, directing me to the homes of those most in need after
services. This was new territory—for the local congregation,
for me, and for the regional church governance watching our
experiments in a long-term, part-time pastorate shared among
available bilingual clergy. We had to cross administrative borders
and walk in new directions to meet one another.

What transformed me most was preaching for and with this congregation. Knowing that some of the girls and boys in the pews were themselves undocumented, or that their family members were of mixed legal status, I had to preach differently. I talked about the politics of deportation, the laws in Arizona that terrified Latino families in Southern California, and the opportunities and the freedoms that so many were struggling to gain. I started out preaching in Spanish, assuming I was taking up "their language" and respecting the congregation's cultural heritage. But I soon discovered that only the elders understood me. I shifted and began preaching in a more bilingual style—the kind of Spanglish give-and-take that families used in conversation and that children overheard on the soccer field and at gatherings when their cousins, grandparents, aunts, and uncles were together. I spoke directly to them about gangs, bullying, negotiating multiple cultures, translating for their parents, and figuring out what to do if ICE came knocking. As I prepared for the next sermon, and the next, I was reading the stories in Scripture in new ways. I had crossed a different kind of border—an intangible cultural and experiential border that I could only cross because they were teaching me and sharing their stories. Now I heard their voices on every page of Scripture, in the biblical stories of fathers and mothers and children. Here were my congregation's struggles, their questions, their fears, their journeys, and their desire to belong—it was all there. What a gift to be so transformed! Jesus, too, lived at the border; in today's language, he could have been undocumented. I would never have made the connection had this immigrant church not shown me.

Why Does It Matter?

When I asked Santiago to read this chapter for the first time, I tried to explain that I had laid out a composite narrative that followed the basic contours of his life, in parallel to the narrative contours of Jesus's life that Matthew lays out. That made him nervous—but not because of the public exposure. He was nervous that I might be comparing him to Jesus. "Dr. Fogg," he exclaimed, "I'm no savior!"

He's right. Yet I still believe that when we share our stories and hear each other's experiences, we actually connect more deeply to the One who loves us enough to take our human form (see Phil. 2:5–11). Not just my form, but Santiago's form, my neighbor's form—his voice and accent, his skin and hair, her walk, her journey, their immigration. Because I know Santiago, his mother, Maria, and her partner, Angel, I can see the divine in their human forms in ways I never would have if I had remained bounded solely by my own human experiences, speaking only to those who live similar lives to mine.

Santiago is no savior. But his experiences do reveal Jesus. Santiago's suffering may not be a physical cross, but his psychological and legal limbo is taking a devastating toll on his health. His commitment to serve others when he has no security himself is reminiscent of the prophets called to impossible tasks (see Jer. 1:4–13). God often called them to enact in their own bodies the powerless suffering of God's most vulnerable people (see, e.g., Hosea 1:1–2; Ezek. 4:4–15). Santiago speaks of his doubts about God and yet tenaciously clings to a deep sense that God is active in his life, that it is all grace. In Santiago's will to find a way forward, I see Christ as clearly as Easter morning.

I gave Santiago this chapter to read in my office. I got up and made coffee. I looked at my to-do list. I sat back down and tried to grade some papers. I was anxious. This was his story I was telling, and I was anxious to know what he thought. Santiago didn't lift his eyes from the draft for twenty minutes or more. Finally, he looked up and said, "I never saw myself this way before. I didn't know Jesus was like me, that he was an immigrant too. We have to tell people. They think their stories don't matter. You have to tell them their story is like Jesus's story."

3

Vantage Points and Borders—
Where We Stand Shapes
How We See

Mark 12:41–44

Angel's Story

Angel is a man of regular build and medium height who prefers to stand in the background rather than to stand out. He is usually relaxed and quiet and keeps his eyes cast down, although you sense he has energy to spare. When he does speak, his voice is a deep, gruff baritone that surprises me because he uses it so seldom. He is succinct with his words. *Sí* or *no* suffices to answer my conversational inquiries. I had trouble catching all of his words, which makes me think my Spanish must also have sounded strange to him. But we always made an effort to understand each other.

Angel came to our immigrant church through his domestic partner when they moved into the neighborhood years ago.

He helped her raise her kids there, and he worked tending the gardens and trimming the trees of wealthier neighbors. Angel and I regularly exchanged hellos in the church sanctuary or in the fellowship hall courtyard when members gathered around the coffeepot between the English and Spanish worship services. Angel rarely spoke about himself or joined in the group conversations, but he seemed content to be there, part of the gathering.

Angel worked Sundays, so he came to the early service in English while his partner and her grandchildren attended the second service in Spanish. Angel didn't read the English bulletin, nor did he sing the hymns. I'm not sure how much of the English sermon he understood. But even so, Angel had proudly, quietly, and faithfully found his niche in the first service. He arrived each Sunday dressed for outdoor work: jeans, heavy boots, a long-sleeve button-down cotton shirt over a white t-shirt, and a jean jacket. He left his cowboy hat on the back pew. When the time came for Communion, Angel stood at the back of the sanctuary, waiting to carry the elements up to the altar with the ushers, who collected and presented the offering for the day. He picked up the plate of wafers and the cup of wine in his clean but rough and cracked hands. He was never in a hurry. He moved at his own even pace from the back of the church to the front, regardless of the pace the ushers set or the rhythm of the offering hymn.

When Angel handed the elements to me on the dais, he was serving the entire congregation. His action began our preparation for Communion—serving and receiving the body and blood of Christ. Because Christ had served Angel and Angel had served us, I could then turn to serve the rest of the congregation. I loved that order of service, and I loved that Angel bore the elements of Christ's self-offering to the altar. Our hands passed the cup and plate across the railing and we nodded to each other. I turned toward the altar, lifted the elements, and bowed my head. Behind me, Angel backed down the three stairs to the floor, crossed himself, turned, and returned to his seat in the very last pew.

The Church's Story

Angel's church was the small Lutheran congregation of ten to twenty people where I presided at Sunday services once or twice a month. The church stood on a large campus, about half a city block, a consistent reminder of the much larger congregation that had filled all of that space only a generation ago. Demographics had changed, community populations had shifted. Now the congregation was simply keeping the doors open for those who remained. Low buildings ringed an open courtyard. They housed empty classrooms, remnants from when this church was also a school—before either Angel or I had arrived. The last of the low buildings contained a large industrial kitchen next to an auditorium that also functioned as a gymnasium. The church used the wide-open space for congregational Thanksgiving dinners, theater groups, and dodgeball. It hosted the occasional quinceañera celebration and regular community meetings for recovery groups like Alcoholics Anonymous, Overeaters Anonymous, and so forth. It also served as the city's rotating night shelter once a month.

The church complex often felt vacant. Classroom doors and offices were kept locked. They were infrequently used while I was there, compared to forty and fifty years ago, the heyday of confirmation classes, Wednesday night suppers, and active, even heated, church council meetings. Today most of us moved only between the sanctuary and the single fellowship room off the courtyard, while a couple of church council members accessed the kitchen or office as their roles required.

The children and grandchildren of the families who had founded this church and continued to worship there felt deeply the loss of congregants and the changes in their church. Past council presidents, treasurers, choir members, hospitality committee members, and others still with us were aging, and their children had moved away. Once they enjoyed the energy and life of this church; now they endured its decline. Their parents had immigrated to Southern California and grown up in this community, proudly building a church and school to nurture their children. And so it did. Those children were now grown, and some had retired. They had become the parents and grandparents whose children had dispersed throughout the city or had moved out of state or across the nation.

This was an immigrant church. Scandinavian Lutheran immigrants to Southern California founded it—eighty years before I arrived—as an oasis to conserve their cultural identities in America. The church was a place of their own, a place of comfort and security from which to launch a first generation of citizens into the diverse world of Los Angeles in the early 1900s. Then as LA demographics continued to shift, new immigrants arrived, struggled, survived, or moved on, all contributing their cultural gifts, rhythms, and flavors to this town and this neighborhood. In the neighborhoods surrounding the church, a few families of Scandinavian descent remained, as did a few families from the waves of African Americans who had arrived and settled there during the '60s and '70s and then pushed on. By the late twentieth and early twenty-first centuries, Latino populations were the majority in the neighborhood, and a diverse majority at that. Some Mexican families had roots going back generations to a time before this region was even in the United States. Other Central American families were relative newcomers. This is a common story across America's immigrant cities. Each wave of people arrives with their own cultural contribution, but they share the same American dream.

Grasping the complexities of cultural claims, economic stressors, and political and generational tensions—as well as overlapping and intersecting identities—is not easy. In fact, whole fields of academic study are dedicated to understanding these layers of urban identities and the social interactions arising from them.[1] Navigating *between* community identities requires a nimbleness that few of us learn in a formal school setting. For the most part, white or Anglo congregational leaders haven't learned it, and certainly the majority of white pastors have not been trained in navigating between multiple cultural or ethnic identities.[2] To engage human diversity while building communities of faith, one must keep in mind gender, race, and ethnicity as well as social, economic, and linguistic status, generational identity, educational achievement, and even length of residence in particular neighborhoods. Each set of identities manifests itself in particular families and individuals with unspoken expectations, pressures, and gifts[3] that may or may not fit the majority culture assumed on the streets or in their worship experience on Sunday morning.

Vantage Points within Angel's Church

Angel's church held two services on a Sunday morning. The earlier service was in English and followed a traditional Lutheran liturgy, with different settings, depending on the liturgical season, from the printed Lutheran Book of Worship. The later service was in Spanish and combined a free-flowing sermon style with a printed bulletin. We used the same liturgy every Sunday so that the congregation could learn the formal responses through weekly repetition and, eventually, participate from memory rather than attempting to follow a changing bulletin. This made it easier for children, as well as for those who had bad eyesight, difficulty reading, or irregular attendance, to participate. Both forms of liturgy were theologically sound, developed from the Lutheran tradition, and attentive to the preferences of each body of worshipers.

What the congregation may not have realized was that the two services also reflected two distinct vantage points shaped by different cultural identities, levels of literacy, pastoral needs, and past worship experiences. The church had tried but had been unable to build or shape a single, common vantage point from which to worship or govern together. One impediment, or border, was linguistic—few leaders governing in the church were Spanish-speaking. And the youth who were bilingual needed mentoring and training in church polity to be able to serve in leadership roles. Translation in church council meetings was a possibility, but there were also logistical challenges. For example, scheduling a time when working parents with small children (mostly Latino) and retired grandparents (mostly of European decent) could all attend was almost impossible. Age and family responsibilities created additional vantage points whose borders seemed unbridgeable.

Another impediment was financial. The church could not afford a full-time pastor or even a dedicated pastoral staff person who could move between the two language services and mentor leaders in both language communities. Resentment grew when the plate offerings were collected from each service and compared. The vantage point of the English speakers who contributed more regularly in time and money was often invoked to dismiss collaboration with the Spanish speakers, who contributed less time and money. The linguistic, financial, and scheduling lines were drawn, and these borders hardened between people attending different services within the same congregation. Everyone was frustrated.

Where we stand in a community—our vantage point along with its related insights and blind spots—is often related to our privilege. Privilege refers to the access, status, authority, or power some have because of who they are and where they come from. Gender and racial privilege, for example, refer to certain advantages or access to opportunities that others do not have. Educational and economic achievement also bestows privileges that provide us with advantages and opportunities as well. It is easy to take our gender, racial, educational, economic, linguistic, political, or cultural privileges for granted. It seems to be human nature to take advantage of our privilege and to assume that our vantage point is objective. We occupy our places and roles in the world without thinking about how we got there. Because who we are feels like a given, the more privilege we have, the more we fail to recognize that not everyone has the same opportunities that our privileges have given us. When we make decisions and exercise power out of those privileges, we can stumble, offend, and miss the mark we were aiming for because we have only part of the picture. Paying attention to our particular vantage point in our community is one way of checking our privilege. By regularly attending to our own vantage point (where we stand) and privilege (who we are), we remind ourselves that the more people with different vantage points we engage, the more resources and imagination we have together to solve conflicts and problems that affect us all.

In Angel's church, the founding Scandinavian immigrant families exercised an unexamined veto authority in congregational decisions. These members, English-speaking descendants of the founders, had faithfully remained in the church of their grandparents and great-grandparents, and for that reason they felt responsible for continuing and even prospering the legacy of the founders. They were proud of their Scandinavian cultural heritages (Finnish, German, and some Swedish) and of their families' Lutheran tradition. The church buildings, classrooms, and open courtyard defined their childhood and were the touchstones of their identity. In the sanctuary they sang hymns in the languages that their grandparents had spoken at home. They didn't understand all of the words, but they felt that this was their home—this language in this place, this America where they could be *both/and*: *both* Scandinavian, of their ancestral inheritance, *and* American, where they had put down roots.

But the church had changed. Decades before, the Scandinavian immigrants had opened the church doors to other, primarily Spanish-speaking, immigrants. Now the children and grandchildren of the Spanish-speaking members, together with newer arrivals from Spanish-speaking countries, had grown up in the very same church, attending Spanish-language services, singing the hymns in Spanish—the language their parents and grandparents spoke at home with them. They had celebrated their First Communions and attended the baptisms of their brothers, sisters, and cousins and the weddings of their neighbors. They had walked to the church, shared refreshments on the patio, played tag in the auditorium. Their children didn't understand all the words to the Spanish sermons, but many families felt that the church was their home—this Spanish-language service in this place, this America where they could be *both/and*: *both* Latin American, of their ancestral inheritance, *and* American, where they had put down roots.

Conflict was exacerbated when those of European descent made assumptions out of their own vantage points and privileges. The founding families of Scandinavian descent tried to preserve the church as they had known it. They had been raised listening to and participating in Lutheran congregational procedures, committee protocols, and church council governance. But they were frustrated that all of the leadership fell on their shoulders. They tried to get people from the Spanish service onto the governing council and onto the membership rolls so they could vote on budget decisions. But when congregational officers tried to contact Spanish attendees, phone numbers were out of service and mail was returned marked "not at this address." Another point of conflict came over the offering plates. The plates collected from the English service contained neat envelopes of weekly tithes to pay monthly building expenses.

But the offering plates from the Spanish service only contained inconsistent amounts of cash and change—no envelopes. Those of Scandinavian descent concluded that some people weren't pulling their own weight.

My Vantage Point

Seeing the Church

As an outside pastor serving both groups, I saw a different story. First, the Scandinavian leaders had learned over generations that serving and church governance were key to maintaining the church. They had learned to serve on committees, use Robert's Rules, and mentor newer members in those responsibilities. The Spanish speakers had not learned this kind of church governance. They assumed that the responsibility of members was to be baptized, to attend on Sundays, to help out on church clean-up days, and to be married in the church. They did not understand the importance of voting in congregational meetings because most had not been mentored in the culture of congregational decision-making.

Second, the young adults of the Latino families who had been raised in the church had never seen their Spanish-speaking parents serve on the church council or the worship planning committee or as treasurer. Perhaps their parents had not learned because there wasn't a need for more leaders a generation ago, because of the linguistic barriers (bilingual church council meetings can take a lot longer), or for a myriad of other reasons. The young Latinos raised in the church, even though they spoke English, had also not been mentored as young people to learn how their church was governed. So when the church needed their leadership in order to survive, these young people did not have the skills to jump in and help. The solution had been lost a generation ago when the church did not cultivate membership across the linguistic and cultural boundaries and mentor its youngest Latino members in running the church.

A third problem was economic instability. In this church neighborhood, Scandinavian families had moved in one hundred years ago and bought homes or land. Since then, housing prices had risen in Pasadena, as they had all over Southern California. The Latino families who had arrived in the last thirty to fifty years were still renting, unable to buy a house in the neighborhood. So, when a family member lost a job or changed jobs, families had to choose whether to pay the rent, the phone bills, the electric bills, or the food bills—or whether to move somewhere cheaper. When a property owner renovated and raised prices on an apartment complex, families who rented had to pack up and move on short notice, and they didn't always update their mailing addresses. For these and other reasons, many families did not give the church a permanent address or phone number for the membership rolls.

Other families, out of fear for their undocumented status, simply did not give out an address for public distribution, even to their churches. Tithing with church envelopes is a way for churches to keep track of active members. It is also a learned practice that records members' information for public reporting to the federal government. Scandinavian families appreciated tithing envelopes because they could write their contributions off for tax purposes at the end of the year. For undocumented families, providing an address for a tax write-off was far less important than staying off the radar of the federal government.

Yet even with these misunderstandings, I saw people from both services pitch in regularly on Sunday mornings to support both worship services. For example, in the Spanish service Norma came early to welcome people as they sat down. Esperanza listened to the prayer requests during the service and then visited anyone who was in the hospital—whether they spoke Spanish or not. One of the children who arrived at the start of services would light the candles with me. In the English service, Jeff led the hymns and his sister offered special music when she was in town. Debby brought flowers from her garden for the altar. One of our elder members was housebound but still sent a check now and then to cover the cost of coffee for fellowship between services. She wanted the fellowship to continue, even if she couldn't be there to enjoy it. Angel contributed by bringing the Communion elements forward during the service. He was the only adult member of the congregation who regularly crossed the language border to worship and serve in the Sunday service that was not in his primary language.

Seeing Angel

From where I stood on the dais to lead worship on Sunday mornings, it was easy to see that Angel was the only Spanish speaker in the early service. The English speakers sat in their regular pews in the front of the church, while Angel sat in his regular pew against the back wall. Because I knew the congregants, I could also see the differences in their socioeconomic privileges. For example, those sitting in the first three rows had all finished college, held an advanced degree, or were young adults expecting to go to college. They certainly did not have easy lives. They watched their budgets closely, but they also owned their own houses, had insurance, and had set aside money for retirement.

In contrast, I knew that Angel had not finished the fourth grade. I knew he rented a two-bedroom apartment that was home to three adults. And I knew, confidentially, that Angel was undocumented. This meant he couldn't open a bank account to tithe electronically, let alone start an IRA for retirement or take out a business loan. Angel couldn't vote or apply for a driver's license.

Although everyone was happy and comfortable where they were sitting in the church, from where I stood the physical distance between those seated in the front pews and the man seated in the last pew mirrored symbolically the linguistic and socioeconomic distances that yawned between the church's English-speaking immigrant families and the Spanish-speaking immigrant families.

But I could also see, from my vantage point on the dais, that the socioeconomic and linguistic distances were not the final word for our worship community. Parents of both sets of immigrants worked or had worked cleaning other people's houses, serving as office janitors or as gardeners. A number of those in the front pews had started their own businesses. Angel, too, was an entrepreneur. Like many immigrants, including the founding church families, he had filled a niche in the local economy where there was a need and he could answer that need. Angel had built his own landscaping business and provided for his partner and her son. He did not own his home, but he regularly gave to the church and volunteered to help out with the grounds and maintenance. How was it that more of us in this church didn't see the common ground, the shared resources, and the contributions as well as the differences in privilege?

At that moment, three things gave me an edge. First was my physical vantage point: I was facing the congregation, and they were all facing me, seated in horizontal rows oriented toward the altar. Second was my professional vantage point. I had access to private information from confidential, pastoral conversations, and I could move back and forth across the linguistic boundaries that many of the congregation could not. This meant that I could listen to every member of the congregation in the language that was most comfortable for them. It also meant that when groups of congregants were speaking, I could easily join in the conversation.

One more vantage point was, for me, also revealing. I was an outsider. I was not Lutheran, so I had to learn how Lutheran congregations practice self-government (no polity is self-explanatory). I had to recognize and articulate my assumptions about how things "should" work and then learn how this congregation did things, what their assumptions were. I had to ask questions. I had to learn from everyone who was there. I had to observe and listen. And, as an outsider, I was expected not to know—which made it easier to ask questions—and people did not assume that I should know.

Seeing Communion

One of the things I observed was that although Angel carried the elements forward, he never received Communion. After passing the elements to me, he would return to the railing and kneel with arms crossed to receive a blessing. I learned that many of the Latino families in our church had been raised Catholic or had absorbed Catholic teaching as children growing up in Latin America. In Catholic teaching, they had learned that only after First Communion and regular preparation by personal confession does one participate in Communion by taking the bread and the wine. Angel had never celebrated his First Communion. And now, since the church did not have a permanent pastor, there weren't any adult Communion classes offered, and there was no one to meet with Angel during the week for Communion instruction. So even though he brought the Communion elements from the back of the church up the steps to the altar, Angel did not receive the body and blood of Christ during our celebration of Communion.

I remember the Sunday morning when I finally put together all of these observations, gathered from my unique vantage points, and understood the importance of Angel's Communion offering for this congregation. As insights often do, this one came with a change of routine. For a year or two after I arrived as pulpit supply to lead services, I always found the altar set and ready for Communion, the elements waiting at the back of the church with the offering plates, fresh flowers in the vases, and bulletins stacked at either entrance of the church. I came to take this for granted. Then one Sunday someone new set the altar and arranged the elements for Communion before the service began. The new altar dresser was a woman named Lucy who worked Sundays for a prison ministry and could not attend worship with us, her home church. So she volunteered to stop by on her way to work to set up the Communion elements, flowers, and bulletins before the first service. Another part-time pastor who was Lutheran took the time to train Lucy in setting up the altar.

On the same morning that Lucy started her service at the altar, I arrived late (blaming the LA traffic, I'm sure) and rushed to lead the first service. I quickly robed and grabbed the liturgical book, hymn book, sermon, bulletin, hand sanitizer, pen, and list of prayer requests I had just been handed. I moved behind the altar and set the liturgy down. As the opening music began, I registered for the first time that Lucy had beautifully arranged all of the Communion elements right there in front of me on the altar. I took the whole setting in. She had draped the chalices of grape juice and wine with linen cloths placed just so; the Communion wafers were covered, set correctly to the side of the chalices, ready for service. It was perfect. But, I then realized, how would Angel bring the elements *from the back of the church* when they were already on the altar? How could he share in the elements of Communion?

I looked out at the congregation and saw Angel faithfully sitting in the last pew. I saw the offering plates waiting at the back of the church for the offertory music. No Communion elements back there. Suddenly the ritual felt off. But the music had already started. There was a moment of confusion in my head. I shook it off and walked to my pew to sit, signaling the beginning of worship.

Making Choices

As worship leader that morning, I had a few options. I could have simply walked the Communion elements down the aisle to the back of the church and let the music continue until I was finished. Then Angel could bring the elements forward with the offering at the right time. I could have later conferred with Lucy and the other supply pastors to work out an adjusted protocol for the elements that included both Lucy and Angel. We could have invited Angel to work with Lucy on the setup of the altar. We could even have coordinated and planned a First Communion class and service for Angel. I'm sure there were other options. In the end, my choice felt anticlimactic: I simply brought the dilemma to the attention of the other supply pastors to address. There are many ways to incorporate the gifts of all the members of the community, but first we have to see them. And where I stood that morning helped me to see both the contributions of others and the importance of my vantage point in calling attention to some of the needs of the congregation that were not visible to others.

Our vantage point—where we stand in relation to others—shapes what we can and cannot see. Standing in the different vantage points of an outsider on the periphery, a member in the middle, or a worship leader who faces everyone can yield different insights on what is happening in the intricate, often invisible or routinized interactions of a community. But where we stand can also impede our vision. That Sunday morning I could see what was happening with the Communion elements *because* I was standing on the dais, facing the congregation. Those in the pews could not see the same dynamics. Because I attended both services and could communicate with both Spanish and English speakers, I could note some cultural differences and similarities between members that they themselves could not appreciate from where they stood. From the professional vantage point of a pastor, I could recognize that there were some economic and class boundaries, generational gaps, and borders created by our cultural and racial assumptions.

Jesus Navigates Vantage Points, Privilege, and Choice

In that moment of staring at the perfectly aligned Communion elements, I felt that Angel had been somehow cut off from touching the body and blood of Christ. I realized that my vantage point—and what it allowed me to see—came with a responsibility. I could choose to teach, share, ignore, or invite others into my vantage point. And I could choose to seek out the insights of others from their vantage points.

Jesus himself offers a picture in Mark 12:41–44 of how to make a choice about exercising or limiting our own privilege, how to stand with new awareness in a particular vantage point, and how to invite others to stand with us and have new insights.

The story takes place in the Jerusalem temple, built on a high hill overlooking the city. Here Jesus engages the crowds that have come to the temple for Passover. He argues with political leaders and religious leaders (12:13, 18, 28). He speaks in parables and answers questions. He warns against "the scribes, who like to walk around in long robes and to be greeted with respect in the marketplaces" (12:38). He teaches his disciples. Rarely do we consider where Jesus physically positioned himself while speaking. But Mark mentions that, at the end of the day, Jesus sits down "opposite the treasury" (12:41). This is the vantage point from which he speaks in Mark 12:41–44.

The temple treasury was located within a matrix of concentric courtyards. The temple courtyards were constructed to guide the faithful from outside the temple gates inward through progressive interior spaces organized by "ascending height and degree of holiness."[4] In other words, Jewish worshipers climbed up the hill to the temple and then moved from the outer Court of the Gentiles into the Court of the Women, then farther up and into the Court of the (male) Israelites, and finally up and into the Court of the Priests. The farthest, highest, most interior, and most restricted area inside the temple was the holy of holies itself, where God's throne was located, and access was restricted to the high priest. The entire temple structure was built to convey that the holier one was, the closer one could come to God's throne.[5] In this way, ethnicity, religious identity, gender, and religious roles all contained privileges that gave people access to or kept them from entering and standing in a particular vantage point in the next courtyard.

Each courtyard had a specific function that roughly corresponded with the role and place of those who had access to it. So, for example, Gentiles could only enter the temple complex as far as the Court of the Gentiles. Commerce took place in that courtyard. People bought and sold small animals and exchanged Roman coins for temple coins to make their offerings. Only Jews could pass through the Court of the Gentiles to enter the Court of the Women. The treasury was located there, and many teachers, like Jesus, held discussions in that courtyard. Jewish women and children could stand in that area and make offerings but go no farther. Any circumcised Jewish man could leave the Court of the Women and move into the smaller, more intimate Court of the Israelites. But only the priests could enter the Court of the Priests. Entering a courtyard beyond one's privilege could result in death.[6] Everyone in the temple grounds, including Jesus and his disciples, followed this system of religious privilege articulated in the concentric courtyards. The courtyard walls reinforced the message that Gentiles were less holy than Jews, women were less holy than men, and Jewish laymen were less holy than the appointed priests.

So where did Jesus choose to stand in the temple? What privileges did he exercise as a Jewish man? What privileges did he refrain from exercising?

According to Mark's Gospel, Jesus did not go up to Jerusalem to visit the temple until the final weeks of his life.[7] Jesus's ministry focused on the people who lived away from the purity restrictions and formal rituals of the temple. But, as Passover neared, Jesus and his disciples joined Jewish pilgrims from all over the empire and made their way to Jerusalem (Mark 11:1). Even though they arrived late in the day, Jesus and his disciples trekked up to the temple, entered, and "looked around at everything." Then Jesus led them down the mount and out of Jerusalem to Bethany, where they stayed the night with friends (11:11).

On his second day in Jerusalem, Jesus took his disciples back up to the temple (Mark 11:15). They entered the Court of the Gentiles, where the temple commerce was taking place. This vantage point matters. The crowds gathered in that courtyard were from multiple ethnicities, classes, genders, and religious statuses. In the midst of all the commercial activity, Jesus overturned the tables of the money changers. Because he was in the Court of the Gentiles, Jews and Gentiles, businesspeople, entrepreneurs, beggars, and pilgrims heard Jesus's teaching and witnessed his prophetic act.[8] Had he gone farther into the temple, he would have occupied a space that left the Gentiles out of his teaching. It is unclear how long Jesus's prophetic action interrupted the buying and selling in the Court of the Gentiles (11:16), or to what extent. Mark adds that Jesus was teaching while he disrupted the commerce (11:17),[9] that the crowds were "spellbound," and that the chief priests and the scribes "kept looking" for a way to kill him. In the evening, Jesus and his disciples left the city (11:18).

On the third day, Jesus returned to the temple, walked around the courtyards, and began teaching again (Mark 11:27). Mark does not specify where Jesus stood while he was teaching on the third day. But it is likely that Jesus and his disciples had made their way through the Court of the Gentiles, with its loud haggling, market hawking, and noisy animals, into the next courtyard—the Court of Women—where arguments and discussions among Jewish leaders traditionally took place. Mark writes that Jesus engaged scribes, chief priests, elders (11:27), Sadducees (12:18), Pharisees, and Herodians alike (12:13). When these leaders tired, others appeared, and through it all the crowds listened "with delight" (12:37).

After Jesus criticized scribes for their showy wealth and claims of privilege (Mark 12:38–39), he sat down in the Court of Women "opposite the treasury" (12:41). Here, Jesus's vantage point is clear and quite different from the Court of the Gentiles the day before. The Court of Women was open to Jewish families, including men, women, and children, but noisy merchants remained outside. Jesus's teaching about Torah and finer points of faith and practice was appropriate to this context—Jewish arguments meant for Jewish worshipers, rather than a prophetic act that a wider audience, including Gentiles, could perceive.

From his vantage point opposite the treasury, Jesus then observed the crowd. He watched "many rich people put in large sums" (Mark 12:41). But he drew his disciples' attention to the widow who "put in two small copper coins, which are worth a penny" (12:42). He told his disciples, "This poor widow has put in more than all those who are contributing to the treasury. For all of them have contributed out of their abundance; but she out of her poverty has put in everything she had, all she had to live on" (12:43–44). Unlike the wealthier Jewish patrons and religious leaders, the widow did not put on a show or try to attract attention; she did not seek public praise. Her offering was financially worth much less than any rich man's patronage. Yet Jesus declared her two coins far greater than the most lavish donation that had cost the wealthy patrons relatively nothing.

Two points are important here. First, in his final day of teaching in the temple, Jesus limits his privilege. That is, he remains in the Court of Women and does not enter the Court of the

Israelites, which was reserved for circumcised males like him. If he had exercised his full privilege as a Jewish male and entered the Court of the Israelites, he might have missed the widow's offering. It is by limiting the exercise of his own privilege that he can lift up the widow's copper pennies as an example of giving one's whole self to God (Mark 12:43–44). At the same time that Jesus makes choices about exercising privilege in this story, the widow does not have the same privilege or choices available to her. Her gender identity confines her to the Court of Women. She cannot move any closer to God's throne within the existing temple system. Still, she gives all she has from her vantage point, and it is more than the wealthy, circumcised men give (12:41, 44).

Second, Jesus's privilege gives him access to both the Court of the Gentiles and the Court of Women. He leverages his privilege to enter both courtyards and teach Gentiles as well as his own people. Each vantage point offers a different audience and also elicits different critiques and actions from Jesus (interrupting commerce and teaching on day 1, then teaching and observing on day 2).

The exercise of privilege and the restriction of privilege is a balancing act. On the one hand, leveraging one's privilege permits certain vantage points unavailable to others. Limiting one's privilege permits other vantage points. When, like Jesus, we do not leverage or take advantage of a privileged position or role, we have an opportunity to see the world from a different, and often valuable, vantage point—that of our neighbor.

In the Court of Women, Jesus teaches his disciples a lesson about economic privilege. He points out the irony that a widow with very little privilege or social value gave everything she had while wealthy men of great privilege and social value gave only a fraction of their worth. Although the treasury was placed in the Court of Women to receive offerings from all Jews, the public nature of these offerings allowed the economically privileged to show off that status. Jesus does the opposite, curtailing his own privilege and lifting up the widow as an example to teach his disciples. By doing so, Jesus publicly challenges the privilege enshrined in tithing practices and ritual offerings. In the Court of Women he invites the disciples not just to reorder how they value gifts and offerings to God, but how they value the giver. While in the eyes of some the widow was one of the least valuable people at the treasury, Jesus insists that the disciples see her offering, her presence, and her great value before God.

Learning from Jesus's Choices in the Church

From my vantage point on the church dais, I could see Lucy's offering—her careful placement of the Communion elements. I could see the offerings of the other part-time pastors doing their best to lead worship. I could see the offerings of the individuals who were present, and I knew that what they gave, and what their families had given, was more valuable to them than I could understand.

I could also see what would have been Angel's weekly offering on the altar before me—his copper pennies. I could see the collection plates through the eyes of the wider community who did not know Angel or the Spanish-speaking members personally. Some saw Angel as a "poor widow" figure—just an immigrant gardener who didn't speak English or bring economic value to the church. But this church had also witnessed Angel bear the body and blood of Christ to the altar as he served the congregation. Angel, like the poor widow, gave his whole self in our worship service so we could all come to the table. He arrived faithfully, even on that morning when he wouldn't be able to touch the body of Christ.

Across the US, some Christians look around their neighborhoods and see illegal immigrants rather than brothers and sisters in Christ. They assume that immigrants can't contribute, that they only take resources. Some complain about immigrants stealing American jobs. Others are upset at recent arrivals who "refuse" to assimilate or learn English. I have heard all of these lines, even from Christians, even in Angel's congregation. To all these people I offer Jesus's example in the Court of Women, where he limited his own privilege in order to witness and lift up the widow's offering. She only gave two pennies, but from where he stood, Jesus could see that she was giving everything she had (Mark 12:44).

Summarizing the Challenge

The story of the widow's offering reminds us to think carefully about where we stand in relation to the whole people of God. It reminds us, as disciples, to look carefully where Jesus directs our gaze. Jesus's choices remind us to stand in public places that are accessible to all kinds of people. For example, one of the pastors on our part-time team regularly served Communion on the sidewalk out in front of the church. She offered Christ's consecrated body or just talked, prayed, or blessed people as they walked by. This is one vantage point that Jesus also occupied—outside the entrance to the temple—that was available to everyone, including Gentiles, women, and children.

The widow's offering also reminds us that many people are bringing their whole selves to God, even when their purses are practically empty. Priests and congregational leaders are often too interested in the "sacrifices" that attract attention. Seeing the widow from Jesus's vantage point, we remember to honor all gifts to the treasury. Even more importantly, we can practice paying attention to the multiple ways people offer themselves in service to the church, to each other, to their neighbors, and—in all these ways—to God.

From where I stood presiding at Communion, I could see the back of the church while the congregation faced the front. How often do we invite people to turn around? To stand somewhere else? To face the four corners of the earth? To stand in a circle and face one another? To move out onto the sidewalk? How do we exercise and teach our responsibility to draw attention to those rendered invisible by certain privileges and vantage points? How do we lift up the multiple ways of giving in our midst?

Priests and lay leaders can mentor the next generation of leaders by creating access to the altar for people, by supporting their varied contributions to the congregation, and by publicly recognizing the equal status before God of every individual and family. Shared congregational responsibilities invite people to respect others and to celebrate one another's dignity as they serve.

How can we train, empower, and call Jesus's disciples forward for specific responsibilities in our churches so that they experience belonging and contribute to the whole body? Angel's story illustrates the important role the congregation has to discern boundaries and bridge them. Pastors and leaders can do some of this work from their designated vantage points. But everyone in the congregation can learn to reflect on and gather insights from their unique vantage points and roles. Angel bridged linguistic borders to attend the English service, and this helped me to see that there were borders within our worshiping community that divided well-meaning people. The challenge today is for us to follow Jesus's lead to intentionally limit and leverage our privilege and to change our vantage point so that we can see our sisters and brothers—like the widow, like Angel, and like so many immigrant Christians—who are giving everything they have in service to God.

4

Challenging Border
Wall Mentalities

Ruth and Mark 7:24–30

This chapter takes a look at the borders of gender, ethnicity, and privilege—and where these intersect one another—to ask what happens when people enter into conversation across these borders and intersections.[1] Because I am engaging other people's stories from my own vantage point and experience, I also tell a bit of my own story to be clear about who I am and where I stand in relation to the women whose stories I share.

Women's Stories: Their Lives and Choices

In 2017, I was invited to speak on the topic of "Women in the Reformation" at the Latinx Symposium organized by the Southwest California Synod of the Evangelical Lutheran Church in Glendale, California. It was a two-day gathering with plenary talks and workshops in Spanish and English with bilingual translation available. Present were many Latina Lutherans and Baptists from around the greater Los Angeles region, as well as representatives from sister congregations in Ecuador. Among the mostly lay women leaders and attendees were a handful of ordained Latino pastors (they had accompanied their congregants) but only one or two ordained Latina pastors. The majority of the participants were working-class women—mothers, daughters, grandmothers, aunts, and sisters. The scheduled speakers were an activist, a theologian, a historian, a biblical scholar, a choral director, a musician, and the regional Lutheran bishop.

Gender in My Story

Although the room was full of women, I observed that most of the men who were present held positions of privilege and authority—from the male bishop to the (majority) male pastors. This dynamic of lay women led by male pastors always makes me edgy. It's not just that I'm an anomaly here as an ordained woman. It's also the knowledge that my mother's and grandmother's generations had to challenge church authorities to be admitted into the circle of ordained ministers and elders. Those women had heard God's call to ministry, but male religious authorities were the gatekeepers, and they maintained the border walls that kept women from ordained church leadership.[2]

This gender dynamic raises personal memories of exclusion for me. I flash back to conversations with a male elder who told me he could not support my application to the pastorate, even though I had been a member of my home church longer than he had. I remember a conversation with a fellow seminarian who told me that women who teach or preach defy the Word of God. I also remember the male students who called me "professor" in class my first year of teaching, but who also made a point to tell me they were boycotting my ordination service in our campus chapel, even though I would be the first person ordained there, because they didn't believe I should be ordained to Word and Sacrament. These were all Christian men who took Communion *with* me but preferred not to receive Communion *from* me. It makes me wonder if a few of the people who walked out during one of my sermons in recent years did so because I addressed "political" subjects (the reason they gave) or because I was a woman voicing perspectives with which they disagreed.

Race in My Story

While I have learned the ways my gender can function against me in leadership roles, I have also learned the many ways in which my race, education, and class function in my favor. Most of the men and almost all of the women at the symposium were Latino/a/x. I am white and was a guest speaker. Although I knew I had come to this symposium on "Women of the Reformation" to speak as an ally of the Latina women present, my gender was not enough to overcome the differences of race and class. White allies like me have their limits—their boundaries, if you will. For example, I had not experienced firsthand the day-to-day racism, xenophobia, or ethnic backlash these Latina women and their families have experienced. I had not felt the fear so many undocumented people in Latinx communities feel on a daily basis across the country.

I also know that (however unintentionally) my presence can change the dynamics of what and how laypeople and people of color are willing to share—just as the presence of a group of majority male pastors shifts my own consciousness and self-awareness. A wise colleague once reminded me that "this is the work." He meant that being allies across racial, class, and gender distinctions requires a willingness to work together outside of our comfort zones. For white, cisgendered, educated people like me, this work requires humility, vulnerability, and a willingness to be uncomfortable as we learn new ways of being partners in our communities. The work requires that we be willing to make missteps and mistakes and learn from those whose voices have been underrepresented. Those of us who wish to be allies must recognize the limitations of our vantage points and privileges. If we seek to be white-allies, scholar-allies, or educator-allies, we can come ready to offer our expertise and skills when invited, but we must also come willing to be transformed by the conversation and by all the community members who are present. Rather than hide behind our expertise or skills, we must commit to being voices in the conversation, remembering those whose voices are not represented.

Women's Stories at the Symposium

I arrived early to the symposium, and within a half hour the women began arriving. Soon they were everywhere, pulling food from boxes and bags; uncovering plates of sweet breads, donuts, and fruit; and opening giant thermoses of *horchata* and *agua de jamaica*. Synod staff women were setting up coffee makers, napkins, paper plates, and insulated cups. The male staff members and pastors set up the tables. Then they chatted, standing in the center of the room with their coffee and sweet bread, telling stories and catching up. The women also chatted as they continued to work, setting out the food, directing new arrivals, arranging and shifting items. I helped out where I could and introduced myself here and there. I pointed people to restrooms, set up more chairs, met the other speakers, and caught bits and pieces of shared stories as I moved around.

Many of the women were third- or fourth-generation US citizens. Others were from mixed-status families—they had some family members with legal documentation and some who were undocumented US residents. A number of the women had finished high school, but many had not. A few of the women spoke English, but many more spoke mostly Spanish. Conversations among the women drifted to stories about immigration and deportation. I overheard the participants mention relatives in Mexico or Central America, family members they had not seen in decades. They exchanged stories and laments of being here in the US when their mothers or grandfathers passed away in Mexico. They commiserated that they hadn't been able to care for an aunt who was sick in Guatemala, or an older sister who had returned to El Salvador. These women were the caretakers of their families, and without legal documentation or the finances for travel, they had to choose whether to stay with the daughters they were raising north of the border or to attend to the ill and dying south of the border. If they chose to cross the border to be with the elder generation, they might be unable to cross back to the US to raise the next generation. I listened to their stories—confessions, really—as they mourned their aging relatives who died alone in the south. Over coffee and sweet bread these women embodied the priesthood of all believers, hearing one another's confessions at a different communion table. They recognized each other's impossible choices and offered each other a kind of emotional absolution.

The Unfolding History of Border Crossing

There was a time when such confession and absolution was not necessary. A few decades ago it was easier to cross the US-Mexico border. Breadwinners could migrate north, fill the labor needs in US agriculture or construction, and then return home to Mexico every three to six months to see their children, their parents, and their loved ones. Because working men could cross the border easily and US employers needed them, laborers did not worry about going home to visit their families in the south or returning to work up north. Border crossing was a long commute, but for the most part, families held together. The ease of border crossing began to change in the 1980s and '90s. Then, in the 2000s, fathers and husbands—the breadwinners of their families—could no longer afford the financial cost of paying a smuggler to get them across the border more than once. They could not risk the increased physical difficulty of walking across deserts for days to get back to a job north of the border. So Mexican husbands and fathers stayed in the US, often for years at a time, sometimes for decades.[3]

These laborers faithfully sent money back to their families, but they were lonely. The young men craved intimacy and community, and so many of them started second families. Of necessity, they sent less money back to Mexico, dividing their earnings between their two families. When support from the north inevitably dried up for the first family in Mexico, finances there tightened. At the same time, economic circumstances in Mexico worsened. Wives and mothers could no longer support themselves and their children. There wasn't enough work in the countryside.[4] Now they had to make a choice: go north and cross the border to work and send money home to support their children, or stay with their children in Mexico and slowly starve. The mothers headed north, sometimes taking along an older child who could make the journey and leaving the youngest children behind with neighbors or grandparents. They thought it was just for a few months, or a year or two.

After five or ten years, the children who had been left behind were old enough to set out on their own and seek their mothers, whom they barely remembered, or their fathers, whom some of them had never met. The children who left home to find their parents in the US started a wave of "unaccompanied minors" coming from Mexico to cross the border into the US. They came in such large numbers that we could only call it a crisis. Like the hungry crowds Jesus fed on the hillside, the children kept coming. They left lives of poverty with their grandparents, who could barely provide for them. They left abusive stepparents, or neighbors who had their own children to raise and feed. These child migrants fled neglect and lack of education. They sought the loving parents they dreamed of and longed for but only vaguely remembered. Then, in 2016, just as the tide of unaccompanied minors had slowed and the immigration rates from Mexico fell to their lowest levels in decades, the Trump administration came into office.[5]

Fear of Deportation

In 2017, all of the women gathered at the synod symposium were worried about the new Trump administration. Whether they were undocumented mothers of citizen children, or the documented mothers of recently arrived undocumented relatives, or the documented children of undocumented parents, they were all scrambling. Every undocumented mother was making plans for her citizen children to stay in the US in case she were to be deported.[6] Every legalized family member was helping neighbors, cousins, aunts, and uncles to secure the futures of citizen children if ICE (Immigration and Customs Enforcement) detained their parents. Families began legal procedures to establish shared custody so their children would have adult advocacy in the US. They attended "know your rights" workshops, traded information and gossip equally, and moved in circles of widespread fear. Even if they were to be deported, they had to make sure their children stayed in the US to finish school. Yet how could they possibly leave their children behind? And if they all left the US together, how could they feed and raise their children in their home country without work, without family, without a social network?

At the time of the symposium, churches and other local community organizations were only beginning to tackle the complexities of families divided by deportation. Pastors, schools, child services, and other organizations tried to respond as ICE began widespread arrests of parents and breadwinners. Women at the symposium shared that this was the first time they had been outside their homes in weeks. They were afraid to get groceries, walk their children to school, or show up for work. They feared for their children's safety. They feared for their own safety. What if an immigration raid found them, or ICE picked them up at the public school drop-off? Even in California, a "sanctuary state"[7] that supports the rights of all residents within our state borders and that had agreed not to aid federal ICE agents, a number of longtime resident family members were deported in the first one hundred days of Trump's administration.

Stories of Border Crossing and Boundaries

All of these worries and fears were present as we gathered in the plenary room to begin the symposium. The bishop officially opened the day with prayer and a blessing. I was third in the lineup and had been asked to speak for an hour, including a time of Q&A discussion. My specialty is the first-century, New Testament times, but the gathering was focused on the 500th anniversary of the Reformation. I had decided to begin with the dissolution of the borders of ecclesial authority that began in the Reformation before I shifted to biblical history.

I first observed that Martin Luther had taken the Bible from the dusty library of the papacy in Rome, translated it into the everyday language of the people, and put it directly in their hands. When he bypassed the educated class and the ecclesial leadership, Luther broke down long-standing medieval borders of privilege. This created a need to build schools and educate the people so they could read the Bible, which was now accessible in their common language. This desire for education is something Latinx and other immigrant communities share today; education is still a key to knowledge and economic access.

Second, I mentioned that Martin Luther and his wife, Katharina von Bora, dissolved another border of authority between the church and the family. They moved prayer, Christian teaching, and hymns out of the central church and put these tools of learning and worship in the hands of mothers in their own homes. They raised up the role of mothers, who became teachers of the Christian faith to their children. By dissolving the catechism privileges of a priestly male hierarchy that had limited people's personal access to the divine, the Reformation opened up the Christian faith to the laypeople who followed it.

Today, because of these Reformers, we hear the Word of God in multiple languages—English, Spanish, Korean, Russian, Hindi, Arabic, Portuguese, and so on. The Reformation eventually led women to take leadership roles in the faith. Mothers, aunts, and sisters still teach their children to pray and sing at home. And all of us, the Lutheran "priesthood of all believers" or, in my Presbyterian tradition, "ministers" in the world—both lay and ordained—tell Jesus's stories in our own idioms, in relation to our own experiences. Because of the legacy and work of Reformers like Martin Luther and Katharina von Bora, today we hear and weave Jesus's stories through the fabric of our own linguistic, ethnic, and familial contexts. And we can draw on these stories to understand and address the injustices we encounter in our world today.[8]

Scriptural Stories of Border Crossing and Boundaries

To do this, I told the plenary, we would focus on two biblical stories: one from the life of Jesus's female immigrant ancestors

(Ruth and Naomi), and one from a time when Jesus crossed a border and reluctantly entered into conversation with a stranger (the Syrophoenician woman). I then retold the stories in Spanish and in English, offering commentary, historical background, and brief descriptions of the original cultural contexts as we went along. I wove the biblical stories through contemporary idioms and chose details that touched on the perspectives, concerns, and conversations these women had been sharing earlier in the morning as we gathered.

The Story of Ruth and Naomi[9]

The first story I shared was the biblical story of Ruth and Naomi. Participants were familiar with this story from Scripture and from their own lives. Ruth is the story of a mother and a daughter-in-law who cross borders, lose their husbands, immigrate and emigrate, and ultimately help each other survive even though they are not blood relatives.

Ruth is the daughter-in-law. She is a Moabite woman who leaves her father's house to marry a recently arrived immigrant to her town. Her betrothed is a Jewish man, the son of Naomi. Although they are of different ethnic backgrounds, Ruth joins the immigrant Jewish man's household. She moves in with a Moabite sister-in-law, a Jewish brother-in-law, and a Jewish mother-in-law and father-in-law. The six adults live as what we today might call a mixed family: four immigrants and two locals who are bound together by marriage.

But before the young couples have children, tragedy strikes. The male breadwinners fall ill and die, one after the other. This is quite a blow to the family—Ruth's husband, brother-in-law, and father-in-law are all gone. Left without a head of household, the three women must decide what they will do. Will they stay together in Moab? Will they split up so the two young women can start new families? Who will care for the mother-in-law, Naomi, an immigrant with no relatives in Moab and no social network to speak of, and who is too old to marry or to bear children?

Each woman makes her own choice. Ruth's sister-in-law returns to her father's house, to "her people and her gods" in Moab (Ruth 1:15). She will likely marry again and start a new family. Ruth's mother-in-law, Naomi, decides to return to her Jewish kin in Judah, where she at least has a social network, if not financial resources. These two women make similar choices to simply return home to their own people to start over. They will be reabsorbed into their respective families and cultures of birth. Ruth, however, makes a different choice. She opts to migrate—to leave her home in Moab and travel to Judah with Naomi. For this journey, Ruth binds herself to her mother-in-law, saying,

> Do not press me to leave you
>   or to turn back from following you!
> Where you go, I will go;
>   where you lodge, I will lodge;
> your people shall be my people,
>   and your God my God.
> Where you die, I will die—
>   there will I be buried. (Ruth 1:16–17)

Ruth's words capture the resolute determination of so many migrants across history. She leaves her parents, her sister-in-law, and her people behind. Ruth will help Naomi reestablish Naomi's family line in Judah among the Jews. We remember Ruth for her covenant commitment to her mother-in-law and for her courage to migrate, to trust Naomi's God, and to start a new life among a new people. We also remember this courageous migrant for her descendants, including King David and Jesus of Nazareth.

Reading the Stories of Ruth, Naomi, and the Women of the Symposium Together

Ruth's story is a beautiful one about the faith of our ancestors. But because it is set so far in the past, her story almost makes migrating across ethnic and geographical borders (from Judah to Moab and the reverse) seem easy. Still, as I retold this story in the symposium of Latina women, I got shivers. In the retelling I realized that Ruth's story is a version of the stories so many Latina women had shared that morning around sweet bread and *agua de jamaica*. I could hear new layers of fear, uncertainty, hope, determination, kinship, hardship, and yes, even covenant trust, in Ruth's story—layers of experience Ruth must have had in common with the women participating in the symposium. Ruth's story is not just ancient. It is also contemporary. When I heard the texture of her story alongside the stories the women shared, I began to understand the biblical story more deeply.

First, I became much more aware of the economic difficulties that pushed Naomi to leave her home—twice. Naomi and her husband fled famine in Judah and sought stability for their sons in Moab. They were refugees. Too soon Naomi's husband and sons were dead, and she was forced to leave Moab without an extended family network to sustain her. Again, the prospect of poverty and starvation impelled her to go. Naomi's circumstances remind us to ask about the economic issues that impel our immigrant neighbors to leave their homes and seek refuge in US communities. Then we can dig further and ask how our lifestyles in the US impact the economies of the countries that refugees are fleeing. For example, we could learn how the long-term effects of the North American Free Trade Agreement have affected Mexican migration northward, as well as how conditions created by the drug war impelled Central Americans to flee their homes.[10]

Second, I saw that the biblical story related the reception Naomi had on her return home, but not how Ruth was received in Judah, nor how Naomi and her family were received as refugees in their first move to Moab. Today our newspapers—local and national—fill in that gap. We hear stories of all the negative ways in which immigrants are received in the US. They often suffer racial and ethnic violence, religious targeting, economic disadvantages, and political backlash. Knowing how our brothers and sisters experience these everyday struggles illuminates the gaps in the scriptural stories of Ruth and Naomi. Even more importantly, when we relate the scriptural stories to those of our immigrant neighbors, we are beginning to do the work of hearing our neighbors' voices, honoring their courage, and ceasing to ignore their suffering as just another part of the news cycle. When we hear and take our neighbors' stories and experiences seriously, we can move our communities to concrete action in solidarity with them.

Third, I noticed that the book of Ruth highlights a specific kind of oppression that continues against female immigrants today. The biblical story matter-of-factly names the difficulties poor young women have when they work in the fields, gleaning and collecting the strands of barley that the harvesters leave behind (Ruth 2:8–13). Ruth is able to evade the dangers and violence gleaners experienced in ancient times because a wealthy landowner, Boaz, takes the time to protect her from harassment and sexual abuse by other field hands (2:15–16). But there are few such owners protecting women in the fields today. Immigrant farmworkers—especially indigenous Mixtec women and other Mexican and Central American women working in the US farming industry—risk harassment, sexual abuse, stolen wages, physical injury, and long-term health problems (particularly in pregnancy) from exposure to pesticides.[11] Even if we have not met these contemporary women farmers, the book of Ruth reminds us of their plight.

Ruth also reminds us that we know the work of these women farmers firsthand. They feed us. Their personal risk in agricultural fields across the US puts fresh fruits and vegetables on our tables. Recognizing the connections between the stories of our immigrant neighbors and the stories of our biblical heroes raises our awareness. It can also help us cultivate our compassion for and commitment to stand with immigrant women working in the fields today.

Fourth, the women at the symposium described how critical their kinship ties and extended family networks are to securing the futures of their children, especially if they themselves are deported. Naomi, too, depended on her kinship ties—her social capital—to secure the future of her family once her husband and sons were gone. Indeed, Ruth made a covenant with Naomi beyond the marital kinship that bound them together. Christians can, like Ruth, extend the ties of kinship by making a commitment to raise, clothe, feed, and educate the children whose families are broken by immigration raids, detention, and border separation.

Finally, in Ruth and Naomi's story we see God at work. Naomi, twice a refugee, returns home. Ruth the immigrant follows and is integrated into the people of God. Even in the midst of their family tragedy, loss, separation, migration, and their courage to take great personal and social risk, God blesses the two women.[12] And then, through these two women, God blesses all nations. The Gospel of Matthew reminds us that Jesus descended from Naomi and Ruth, our immigrant ancestors in the faith (Matt. 1:5). Why do we not also ask how God blesses us today through the immigrant women who live as our neighbors, our local farmers, our geriatric caregivers, domestic workers, teachers, doctors, nurses, and local businesspeople?

When Tribalism Gets in the Way

One reason we often do not see the relationship between the divine blessing we receive from our faith ancestors Naomi and

Ruth and the divine blessing we receive from our immigrant neighbors is that human tribal instincts get in the way. Human beings are fundamentally social animals. At our best, we recognize our own; we take care of one another; we share our food, clothes, and shelter. We band together for safety, create complex networks of relationships, mentor one another, and shape a common life together. But the same desire to care for our own can cause us to mistrust and reject strangers. In both instincts—the instinct to care for one another and include others, and the instinct to protect our own and exclude others—we are tribal beings. Sticking together for protection makes us wary of outsiders, people who are different from us, who live differently from us and don't look, sound, or act like our group, our kin, our *tribe*.

So, for example, Naomi and Ruth feel like our people—our faith ancestors. Even though they lived thousands of years ago, belonged to cultures far different from ours, and spoke languages quite distinct from English, we American Christians are taught that the people of God in Scripture are part of our tribe. At the same time, in our current politics, we are told that people who live today on the same continent we live on are foreigners and "aliens" of a completely different tribe.

In Ruth's day, global migration was common. People often assimilated into other human groups and families. But if circumstances changed, those same people could turn on one another and insulate themselves for protection. Today, as we become more aware of global migration, environmental and political refugees, and the push and pull of economic circumstances, we must also recognize our human instincts toward inclusion and exclusion, especially as they manifest in our national discourse. Law professor Amy Chua reminds us, "The tribal instinct is not just an instinct to belong. It is also an instinct to exclude."[13] Acting on that tribal instinct to exclude harms our immigrant neighbors. However, listening to the stories of our immigrant neighbors and entering into conversations with them can defuse our tribal instinct to exclude and help us open our hearts to one another.

The Story of the Syrophoenician Woman

While the book of Ruth does not mention the exclusions of tribalism, we do see tribal dynamics in other biblical stories, even in some of the New Testament stories about Jesus. Looking closely at one of these problematic New Testament stories in conversation with the experiences of the Latina women attending the symposium raises some critical questions for Christians to consider today.

In Mark 7:24–30, Jesus sets off north from the Galilee toward Tyre—a Gentile city on the Mediterranean coast. He leaves his disciples behind in Jewish territory and crosses an ethnic border into Syrian territory. Mark writes that Jesus "entered a house and did not want anyone to know he was there. Yet he could not escape notice" (7:24). Even though he is an outsider in this Gentile region, word has spread about Jesus.

"Immediately" a local woman hears about Jesus.[14] She has a daughter who suffers from an unclean spirit. She leaves her daughter at home and comes to Jesus, prostrating herself at his feet (7:25). Then Mark reveals a potential problem: the woman is a Gentile and Syrophoenician (7:26). That is, she is of a different religion and ethnicity than Jesus. In Amy Chua's words, she and Jesus are from different tribes. For the woman, Jesus's ethnicity is a nonissue. He is on her turf, and she is there for her daughter. She begs Jesus to cast out the demon. He responds rather harshly: "Let the children be fed first, for it is not fair to take the children's food and throw it to the dogs" (7:27).

This rebuke is unexpected. Jesus has not refused to heal a child before. Nor has he used an ethnic slur to drive someone away. Jesus's language was as jarring in the first century as it is today. In his reply, the Jews—Jesus's people—are the "children," and the Gentiles—the woman's people—are the "dogs." How can Jesus say these words? Something is wrong. Why would Mark portray Jesus this way?

Some biblical scholars have dedicated a lot of time to explaining why "dog" is not a derogatory rebuke.[15] But these attempts are not satisfying. Jesus's response in Mark 7:27 is an ethnic slur.[16] His words exclude the Syrophoenician woman and her people from his healing ministry. Similarly, some Christian preachers and teachers have tried to explain that Jesus is simply testing the Syrophoenician woman's faith: he is using the slur to provoke the woman into demonstrating her mettle, showing that her faith can stand up to such a harsh rebuke. But this explanation is also problematic. First, it seems to argue that Jesus didn't really mean what he said. Second, saying that Jesus used an ethnic slur to test a foreign woman's faith doesn't actually solve the problem. The Son of God still uses an ethnic slur. Third, the narrative evidence showing that Jesus was testing the woman's faith comes from Matthew 15:21–28. Mark does not even mention the woman's faith.[17]

There are a couple of ways forward for understanding Jesus's conversation with the Syrophoenician woman. First, we can begin by looking at the broader historical and narrative contexts in Mark.[18] Second, we can read the story of the Syrophoenician woman alongside the experiences of the women who have suffered ethnic slurs and have even been called "dogs" in our own tribal context today.[19]

The Historical and Narrative Contexts

Historically speaking, strong ethnic and religious identities defined people living under the Roman Empire. Although they lived in close proximity to one another, or perhaps *because* they lived in close proximity, first-century Mediterranean people were attentive to the ethnicities, religions, and geographies that distinguished them. People were geographical neighbors, yet dividing lines, bitter stereotypes, and enmities still developed historically and even deepened over time. Such tribal borders often played out in their social interactions or religious restrictions. For example, Jews and Syrophoenicians had a long history of enmity and what Amy Chua might call tribal mistrust acted out in practices of exclusion. First-century Jews kept purity boundaries as well as sociopolitical boundaries between themselves and Gentiles, especially around the Galilee region, where economic pressures on the Jews were particularly high.[20]

Narratively speaking, the Gospel of Mark presents Jesus as the divine, beloved Son of God (1:1, 11; 3:11; 15:39) *and* as fully human. We see Jesus's humanity when he loses patience with his disciples (8:14–21) and when he reacts with amazement that his hometown has rejected him (6:6). We see his humanity when he needs to rest and when he escapes from the crowds to find a quiet place, either alone or with his disciples (6:11, 30–32; 7:24). He feels human emotions such as pity (1:41), compassion (6:34), and love (10:21). He gets hungry (11:12). He grieves (3:5; 14:34). And when the end of his life is near, he becomes "distressed and agitated" (14:33). Jesus does not seem to be omniscient in Mark's Gospel. He does not know what people will do before they do it. He has to ask what people are thinking and often seeks clarification from his disciples (5:30; 6:38; 8:5, 28; 9:33).

For most of Mark's Gospel, Jesus hangs out with his own human tribe, the Jews. In his healing and teaching ministry, he focuses on Jews across the regions of Judea and Galilee. They come from many backgrounds and social statuses. Jesus heals Jewish lepers (1:40–42), casts demons out of Jewish men and children (1:23–26; 9:14–29), calls Jewish disciples (1:16–20; 2:13–14; 3:13), and feeds and teaches Jewish crowds (6:30–44). He spends time arguing with Jewish teachers, leaders, and priests (2:23–28; 4:1–32; 7:1–13; 10:2–9). Jesus visits his hometown of Nazareth (6:1) and then roams among Jewish villages (6:6). He sends his disciples to preach throughout Galilee (6:7–13). Jesus's reputation reaches the political center of Jewish authority in Jerusalem (7:1). Even in the palace, King Herod hears the reports, and he fears that a Jewish prophet, John the Baptist, has come back to life (6:14–29). When Jesus does heal a Gentile, a demoniac from the Gerasene region (5:1–20), Jesus refuses the man's offer of discipleship and instead sends him back to his own tribe (5:19). The man doesn't actually go home but travels throughout the surrounding ten cities to tell Jesus's story to all the Gentiles of the Decapolis (5:20). Still Jesus returns to his ministry with the Jews (5:21).

Like other humans, Jesus needs rest, and he encourages his disciples to rest as well.[21] After sending the disciples out to teach and heal (6:7–13), he invites them away from the crowds, and they go to a deserted place to rest because "many were coming and going, and they had no leisure even to eat" (6:31). When the Jewish crowds catch up, Jesus doesn't turn them away or rebuke them, but patiently teaches them (6:34). When the crowds grow hungry, just as he tended the disciples' needs, Jesus feeds the five thousand families with five loaves and two fish (6:35–44). He shepherds his tribe, the crowds of Jews, whenever and wherever they come to him. He teaches them, feeds them, and heals them. These are his people, and he is available to respond to their needs.

In addition to portraying Jesus's humanity in the Gospel, Mark also presents Jesus discussing the human heart in his public teaching. This teaching on the limits of the human heart directly precedes Jesus's encounter with the Syrophoenician woman. When the Pharisees publicly question Jesus's disciples for not washing before they eat, Jesus uses the opportunity to teach the crowds that nothing outside them can defile or purify them (Mark 7:14–15). Jesus's disciples privately ask for clarification, and Jesus elaborates (7:17–23). The human heart—not external food or handwashing—holds the impurities and evils that defile a person (7:15). Therefore internal purity or defilement is manifested in the words and actions that "come out of a person" and reveal their heart (7:20–22).

After identifying the human heart as the source of evil (and good) words and actions, Jesus leaves his tribe and crosses the border into the Syrophoenician woman's territory. And, in conversation with her, Jesus's negative, exclusivist words reveal something deep within the human heart. Today we might say that Jesus's words reveal human tribal instincts that defile the human heart—prejudices and stereotypes. Thus, within Mark's narrative progression, Jesus easily crosses a geographical border, but he is not able to cross the ethnic border that stands between his tribe and the woman's, even to heal her child.

Then something changes Jesus's words, revealing a transformation in the human heart. Tribal exclusivism does not win in this encounter. Mark's story ends with Jesus observing that the demon has gone (7:30). What happened? A mother's words intervened. The Syrophoenician woman does not let Jesus's rebuke stand unchallenged. She creates a loophole, a way to make the fearful human heart see that there is room at the table for more tribes. She takes Jesus's metaphor about feeding the children and excluding the dogs and she shifts the relationship: she reimagines the household.[22] "Sir, even the dogs under the table eat the children's crumbs" (7:28). In the Syrophoenician woman's metaphor, everyone has a place, and everyone is fed. The table and the household are inclusive.

Jesus responds with new words. "'For saying that, you may go—the demon has left your daughter.' So she went home, found the child lying on the bed, and the demon gone" (7:29–30). Just as Jesus's words reveal the human heart in this narrative, the Syrophoenician woman's conversation with Jesus transforms that heart, and her words open Jesus's ministry. After their conversation, Jesus heads to the Gentile region of the Decapolis

(7:31), heals a deaf man (7:37), and then feeds four thousand Gentile families just as he did the Jewish families (8:6–9). In this transformation of the human heart, Jesus offers us an example of how we humans with our tribal instincts can open ourselves to being changed in conversation with our neighbors.[23]

The Immigrant Women We Have Called "Dogs"

Back in the Latina women's symposium, I paused as I said Jesus's words aloud: "Let the children be fed first, for it is not fair to take the children's food and throw it to the dogs" (Mark 7:27). As I retold the story of the Syrophoenician woman in that context, the word "dogs" stuck in my throat. It hung in the air. It poisoned the space around us.

These words felt most shocking when I pronounced them aloud, in public, in a room full of people who, as immigrants, as Latin Americans, and as women had heard the same insult aimed at them—not a decade ago, but just last week, or on the news, or on their employer's lips, or in line at the checkout counter. I could not, as a biblical scholar, explain away Jesus's words here. I could not tell them, "Oh, Jesus didn't mean it" or "It's just a test." Especially not in today's political climate. Knowing what we know about microaggressions, tribal exclusivism, the impact of internalized racism on self-esteem, and the adverse effects of bullying and even trolling, we need to confront insults that dehumanize our neighbors. We need to recognize the harm these words and attitudes do—whether it is Jesus calling someone a "dog" in Scripture, or a coworker speaking in the office, or a sitting president speaking to reporters. Insulting words reveal the human heart. Spoken aloud, they humiliate and dehumanize people. Such language is painful and meant to exclude. It represents the worst of the human heart and exemplifies the tribal exclusivism that poisons our public discourse today.

I looked at the women before me—the mothers, sisters, daughters, granddaughters, nieces, and aunts. We had talked about the historical context of the story and the narrative context of the story. So I asked them, "What do you think of this Syrophoenician mother?" The symposium hall grew quiet. Perhaps I had said too much, been too critical of Jesus's words. I was the stranger in this gathering. Like Jesus in Tyre, I needed to learn from the women seeking access to the table. Day after day in the news we hear about persistent mothers and fathers who seek healing for their children. They approach the bountiful, but private, US table. The Americans seated at the table are my "tribe," fellow citizens, some enjoying playing the gatekeeper of the border, others afraid that there is not enough bounty in the US for anyone else to even share "the crumbs." In this symposium, I was a white citizen who briefly stepped out of her own territory to enter another's house. These women had mastered the stance of the Syrophoenician woman. They had voiced the anxious concerns of Latina mothers for their family members who needed opportunities, safe passage, and clear legal paths to follow. They had been called dogs—and worse—and had been turned away from the table. They had confronted the walls: border walls, detention center walls, prison walls, educational walls, financial walls, racial walls, and glass ceilings.

What if, I asked them, this Jesus represents the powerful sitting at a table, enjoying a meal while a child is suffering? What if the Jesus in this story represents those who call people seeking help "dogs"? What if it takes a woman from outside this man's own tribe and ethnicity to call him on his exclusivist language, his border walls, his tribalism? If we read the story this way, then Jesus represents the human heart that manifests tribal exclusivism, and the Syrophoenician woman is the hero. She is the one who represents every mother and every stranger who approaches the American table and asks only to share in the crumbs so she can heal, feed, and educate her children.

The Syrophoenician mother embodies the prophetic call of the excluded—all those who are turned away, insulted, or dismissed and yet are precisely the people whose conversation can transform the hearts and minds of those reclining comfortably at the table. Jesus allows himself to be transformed in this conversation with the Syrophoenician woman—a woman and mother just like all of the women and mothers at the symposium.

Following Jesus across Exclusivist Borders

If we read the story this way, Jesus becomes the human exemplar of how to step out of our comfort zones, to cross borders, and to experience transformation in conversation with others who are different from us. If our first reaction to a stranger is to exclude them, Jesus's response in conversation with the Syrophoenician woman shows us that we must reexamine our position. Jesus was willing to be transformed. He recognized the broader mission of divine salvation and healing when this woman presented him with her vision for a shared table. After his conversation with her, Jesus more fully embodied his divinity. We, too, can and should step into uncomfortable territory. We may get it wrong. But we may also find our hearts transformed in conversation with our neighbors.

The symposium ended. But the story of the unnamed Syrophoenician woman lives on in our Scriptures and in the courageous, persistent families at our borders. She lives on in the Latina women immigrants who find the strength and courage to help American citizens open our healing ministries to refugees in need. The women who have crossed the border on behalf of their children continue to suffer the instability of inadequate US immigration laws. They also continue, by their presence, determination, persistence, and expansive vision, to speak truth to power. Their truth is their voice and their presence at our shared table. We need to continually hear their challenging words, which can powerfully transform our humanity. Will we sit back at the table, content to treat others like dogs? Or will we be transformed by conversations with our neighbors that dissolve our tribal boundaries and reshape our human hearts?

5

Letters from
Behind Prison Walls

Philippians 1:12–30

Hugo's Story

The US Department of Homeland Security (DHS) estimates that in 2014, 12.1 million people resided in the country illegally. That is about 3 percent of the total US population. Of those 12 million unauthorized residents, over 75 percent had been living in the US for over a decade.[1] Hugo is one of them.

Chasing the Dream

I first read Hugo's story online at a site called IMM-Print.[2] When Hugo first came to the US at age twenty, he had nothing to lose. Like many young men, he was seeking an opportunity: a solid job, a safe community for his wife, and a stable place for his kids to grow up and go to school. This kind of opportunity did not exist for him in Mexico. Hugo and his wife found work in Northern California, and their children started school. They worked alongside their neighbors, raising their children to be good citizens and to give back to the community.

In 2001, a year or so after he began living his American dream, Hugo was picked up and deported. Back in Mexico, he was desperate to return to his wife and two young children. He would not leave them fatherless, and he knew he could not earn enough money in Mexico to provide for them in the US. So Hugo crossed the border a second time.[3] He did what he could to integrate himself further into the fabric of American society. He secured a tax-identification number and used that to pay his taxes; he obeyed the laws, took his children to school, volunteered with other public-school parents, and regularly attended church. He and his wife had another child, a boy, a citizen born on US soil. Hugo committed himself to working longer hours, after hours, and on the weekends to make ends meet. He worked as a foreman, laying Sheetrock and drywall for his employer, who still calls Hugo one of his best employees.[4] For almost two decades, Hugo lived the life of a working-class American.

Hugo knew he had violated US law when he crossed the border. He does not argue he is innocent. Instead, Hugo presents the case that good people, especially those people who seek to contribute to a safe, clean, respectable, and open community, are precisely the people who are caught almost endlessly in the US detention system at great financial cost to their families and to US taxpayers. Hugo writes,

> I want people to know we are good people. When I came to this country, I was twenty—and I followed all the rules. I paid my taxes and worked hard to support my family. I am a good father and member of the community. We just want to build a better future here for our children and ourselves. I've lived in the US for seventeen years with a clean record. And I'm not

special: there are millions like me out there, all trying to do the right thing. But people like us are powerless to fix our status.[5]

Humiliation, Suffering, and Loss of Status

All of Hugo's efforts to be a working-class American ended on May 3, 2017. Hugo and a coworker reported to work and were given the address of a hospital to start a new job. They didn't realize the hospital was inside Travis Airport Base until they arrived at the gates. At that point, they should have turned around and left. Perhaps they trusted their employer's assignment. Perhaps they misunderstood the limited role of the tax IDs they used. Perhaps it was simply their work ethic: arrive early, do the job, leave only after the job is done. They entered the base and followed the guard's instructions to go to the "visitor center to get a badge and a work permit."[6] At the visitors' center, the military officer on duty did a routine background check and gave the men some paperwork to fill out. Because Hugo did not have a Social Security number, he left that line in the paperwork blank. Hugo later writes, "I told the truth, that I didn't have [a Social Security number], but that I did have a government ID I use to pay taxes."[7] The ID allowed Hugo to pay income taxes while living in the US. But a tax ID is not a work permit, and his lack of a Social Security number was suspicious. The military officer followed protocol and called ICE.

While they sat waiting for ICE to arrive at the Air Force base, Hugo and his coworker called home. Over the phone, Hugo told his wife he was being detained. They both broke down. He remembers that he had to hang up while she was still crying. In just a few short moments, Hugo's status completely changed. He had left home that morning as a dedicated construction worker living the American dream. Now the dream was over. He was leaving work in handcuffs, "with chains around our waists to our wrists, and around our hips, too."[8] In his online letter, Hugo tries to convey the excruciating feelings of that moment. ICE put him in a car, drove him from the town where he was building a future for his family, and delivered him in shackles to a walled facility. "When we got [to the facility] and I saw the fences and guards, I was so scared and confused that I started crying again. It was a prison, and I'd never in my life been in a prison before. I couldn't understand what was happening to me."[9] Hugo's confusion and powerlessness mixed with shame and humiliation as his life and status changed before his eyes. Everything Hugo had worked for disappeared as he entered the walls of ICE custody. His future was in the hands of the guards, the judges, and God. Hugo writes, "I worry every day what tomorrow will bring. But only God knows what will happen."[10]

ICE charged Hugo and his coworker as "foreign nationals attempting to gain entry to the military base."[11] Because Hugo had been deported in 2001 and had reentered the country, he was eligible for immediate deportation. He could not ask for a bond hearing before a judge. With no legal status in the US, Hugo could not even ask for the same rights that any American criminal would expect. Hugo submitted.

I was given a form to sign and told deportations took place on Tuesdays and Thursdays. It was a Wednesday. I signed the form because I didn't think I had a choice. I cried thinking I might be deported the very next day without being able to say goodbye to my family.

I couldn't imagine going back to Mexico and leaving my family behind. And I was scared: I come from a small town in Mexico. The drug cartels are everywhere—it's dangerous.[12]

Hugo's seventeen years of reliable, honest work in the US had no bearing on his status before the law. Nor did the claim that he could not safely return to his home in Mexico. To make a legal case for asylum, he would need a lawyer and a court hearing before a judge. ICE protocols denied him a public advocate. Luckily, Hugo's wife found a lawyer who submitted paperwork in time to contest the detention proceedings and keep him in the US.

If One Member Suffers, All Suffer (1 Cor. 12:26)[13]

Ultimately, Hugo's six-month detention jeopardized his entire family—the people for whom he had risked crossing and recrossing the US border. Hugo's wife and three children suffered emotionally and psychologically. During his first five months in detention, Hugo didn't see his wife, who was working full-time, but he called her each night. Every few weeks Hugo's eldest son and daughter filled the gas tank and drove the two hundred miles round-trip to see him. Hugo remembers, "It's a long trip: visiting hours are from 7:30 p.m.–9:00 p.m., and Rio Cosumnes [detention center] is two hours from [our home], so they don't get home until very late."[14] Hugo's children had difficulty going to school, concentrating, and completing homework. The youngest, the US citizen, was looking forward to celebrating his First Communion. The boy couldn't understand why his father couldn't come to the celebration.

In addition to the frayed emotions and the psychological toll Hugo's detention took on the family, their finances were also stretched thin. Hugo's wife was working as many hours as she could get. But the nightly phone calls cost twenty-one cents per minute. Gas for the two-hundred-mile drive for the kids to visit their father was expensive. The family had to pay the lawyer to fight Hugo's asylum case. And, "because the food is so bad" in detention, Hugo's wife was spending thirty-eight dollars a week to buy Hugo a package of "crackers, instant soup, tuna, and cookies" to supplement his diet. Hugo writes, "In total, my family spends $100 or more a week to meet my basic needs: food, phone calls, stamps and paper." Over just five months, Hugo's detention cost his family $2,000 on top of his lost income. Hugo writes that the worst part is that "I am here [and] I can't do anything to help pay for these costs."[15] Instead of providing for his family as he had for almost two decades, Hugo became their dependent.

Just as the cost of detention rose for Hugo's family, it also continues to rise for US taxpayers. As the number of detained immigrants grows, the US Department of Homeland Security (DHS) hires companies like the GEO Group to run more detention centers across the country and pays GEO $128 a day per detainee.[16] GEO Group then charges detainees twice the retail cost to purchase snacks, stamps, phone calls, paper and pencils, and other basic supplies. GEO Group pays detainees one dollar a day to work in the center's laundry, sanitation department, or kitchen.[17] Many Americans argue that immigrants take our jobs. Ironically, GEO Group advertises that their for-profit detention centers contracted by ICE actually create American jobs.[18] When an immigrant is detained, the financial winner is the GEO Group.[19] Meanwhile, immigration activists and civil rights lawyers are putting together class action lawsuits accusing the US government of contracting slave labor.[20]

In his online letter, Hugo mentioned the various physical deprivations he experienced during his incarceration: lack of sleep, lack of exercise, and no access to the outdoors. "There are a couple skylights, but no windows. We never get to see outside, the sun, the grass, anything."[21] Hugo's letter returns repeatedly to the topic of food and hunger:

> We have to get up for breakfast at four thirty in the morning. A few potatoes, eggs and two pieces of bread, plus milk and margarine. There is a loudspeaker with loud announcements starting at 5:00 a.m. and continuing all day long, so you can never sleep. Lunch is at 11:30 a.m., and is always soup, sometimes

with something in it, and other times mostly just water. Then dinner is at 2:30 p.m. The best food is on Thursday nights at dinner when we get peanut butter and jelly sandwiches.[22]

While a detainee's physical deprivations are striking, the emotional toll weighed on Hugo the most. He felt isolated, disconnected, exhausted, and anxious about the future of his family, and he worried about the outcome of his detention. At the time he wrote and posted his letter online, there was still no clear timeline for his release or even for the legal process to move forward. More than anything, Hugo missed his wife and children:

> Sometimes I'm able to talk to my children [on the phone] too, if they're not asleep, maybe three or four times a week. The other day my youngest son, . . . who's ten years old, asked if I could pick him up from his first day at school. It made me cry to say no. When he asks when I'm coming home, I say, "I'm working. Maybe just a few more days."[23]

Hugo recalled lying to his youngest son in order to reassure him. He was trying to protect the boy from the severity of their family's situation. Hugo had no control over the outcome of detention, but he put on a good face for his family. He encouraged his wife and tried to minimize the fear and disruption in his children's lives. Even in detention, Hugo put his family first, trying to secure their safety and stability. His words were meant to comfort them and to offer some hope in the midst of their anxiety, unknowing, and separation.

Now You Are the Body of Christ . . . (1 Cor. 12:27)

Although I have never met Hugo in person, I know he is my brother, a member of the body of Christ. His online letter to America introduced me to the fear, shame, and isolation detainees experience in our US detention system. Scripture teaches that when one part of the body of Christ suffers, the rest of the body suffers. When people are detained by ICE, often after decades living in the US, they are uprooted from their lives, transported to a new location, and given a new status—an "alien number" instead of a name.[24] Detainees are those who once viewed themselves as honorable, honest, and dedicated family members, working tirelessly on behalf of spouses and children, proudly contributing to this thing we all call the American dream. Now, behind the walls of an ICE detention center, they struggle to comprehend their changed status from "father" or "mother" to feeling like a "criminal." In detention, they are no longer able to contribute to their family's well-being or to help raise their children to be proud American citizens. Instead, they find themselves draining their family finances while the president of the United States calls them criminals, rapists, and "animals" from "shithole countries."[25] People in detention experience this denial of their humanity as an identity crisis. They wrestle with the deeply personal agony of jeopardizing the well-being of their children—the ones for whom they crossed the border in the first place.

Paul's Story

Like Hugo, the New Testament author Paul also wrote a public letter from behind prison walls. Paul was a Jewish resident of the Roman Empire who came from the city of Tarsus. Christians know him as Saint Paul, a successful missionary and an inspirational, if controversial, founder of first-century churches. Paul wrote most of the New Testament letters that we read in worship services, weddings, funerals, and baptisms. There is no evidence that Paul had a spouse or children of his own, but he did refer to those whom he nurtured in Christ as his children (1 Thess. 2:6–8, 11; 1 Cor. 3:1–4).[26] He related to them as a mother might (1 Thess. 2:7; Gal. 4:19) and felt bereft when he was away from them for too long (1 Thess. 2:17). He also wrote that he suffered in order to raise them to maturity in Christ (Gal. 4:12–20), admonishing them as a "father" (1 Cor. 4:14–21) and fighting off the influences of other religious teachers whom he thought would endanger his churches' welfare (Gal. 2:11–12; 5:10–12; Phil. 3:2).

Like Hugo, Paul suffered physically and psychologically. Paul writes that he was detained, imprisoned, flogged, expelled from cities, hungry, cold, anxious, and unable to rest (2 Cor. 11:23–33; Phil. 4:10–14). And, according to Acts and Paul's own letters, Paul endured these difficulties in order to maintain a strong network of Christian congregations across the Roman Empire (Phil. 1:12–14; Rom. 15; Acts 9).

Finally, like Hugo, Paul also crossed borders to reach his beloved family in Christ—his churches.[27] Hugo pursued the American dream with single-minded dedication. And with a similar single-minded dedication, Paul dropped everything at Christ's revelation to pursue only Christ as his goal (Phil. 3:10–12). Taking to the road, Paul crossed borders, traveled through various ethnic territories, and navigated different cultural customs, privileges, legal statuses, and local laws.

Saint, Citizen, or Criminal?

Status matters. Today Christians consider Paul a saint, an apostle, someone set apart by God for a holy mission. Paul has a special status in Christian tradition. But in Paul's own time his neighbors considered him a criminal. They regularly viewed his work as suspicious, socially disruptive, and even illegal. First- and second-century Christian writings report that citizens and townspeople dragged Paul into court for disrupting the social order. For example, Acts 16:20–21 relates the story that local businessmen in the Macedonian town of Philippi brought Paul and his companions "before the magistrates, [and] they said, 'These men are disturbing our city; they are Jews and are advocating customs that are not lawful for us as Romans to adopt or observe.'" Elsewhere in Acts, Jewish leaders accuse Paul before the governor in Caesarea, calling him "a pestilent fellow, an agitator among all the Jews throughout the world, and a ringleader of the sect of the Nazarenes" (Acts 24:5). In another text, written a century later, a leading family of Iconium denounces Paul before the governor for perverting the social order. They claim that Paul convinces young women to break their social contract to marry their betrothed and, instead, to commit themselves to celibacy.[28] For luring young women away from their responsibility to marry and bear children for their families, Paul is bound, imprisoned, and flogged.[29]

Paul also disrupted local economies. Acts 19:22–41 reports that Paul's preaching was perceived to financially undermine the local metal and woodworking unions in Ephesus because he preached so relentlessly against idolatry. The more people followed Paul, the more the market for wooden and metal idols shrank, or so the city's workers feared. Locals accused Paul of disrupting their jobs and putting an entire industry out of work, not to mention offending the local gods (19:23–27). We hear similar charges against immigrants today—that they undermine local economies and take jobs from hardworking American people. Such contemporary voices against immigrants are loud and perpetuate stereotypes, but like that of the mob gathered against Paul in Acts, their rage does not seem to be well founded (see Acts 19:37–41).[30] After the accusations against him were dropped, Paul quickly left Ephesus and moved on to another city (20:1).

A similar reception awaited Paul in Philippi, where he was flogged and imprisoned (Acts 16:19–24; 1 Thess. 2:1–3). In nearby Thessalonica Paul was expelled even more quickly (Acts 17:1–10; 1 Thess. 2:17–18; 3:1–5). In his first letter to the Thessalonian churches he reminds them that "though we had already suffered and been shamefully mistreated at Philippi, as you know, we had courage in our God to declare to you the gospel of God in spite of great opposition" (1 Thess. 2:2). Paul reminds the Thessalonian churches about his difficulties in Philippi to explain that his mistreatment in Thessalonica was not unique. He will continue, and he hopes they will too. Paul fears that if the Thessalonian churches are under too much pressure from their association with him, they won't remain faithful to the gospel (1 Thess. 3:1–5). And, like Hugo, Paul worries that the discrimination, suspicion, and even the humiliations, abuses, and arrests that he has suffered will be extended and inflicted on the communities he loves. He writes letters to strengthen the churches and to encourage them during these troubles and "persecutions" (3:3).

In his imprisonment and prosecution by the civil authorities for criminal behavior, Paul experienced the same humiliation and loss of status that Hugo experienced in his arrest and detention. It is also probable that Paul, like Hugo, lacked citizenship status.[31] Although Acts 22:25–29 presents Paul as a citizen of the Roman Empire by birth, in his letters Paul never claims to be a Roman citizen, to have taken advantage of Roman citizenship, to have requested special treatment, or to have had a hearing before the emperor because of special legal status. Even when listing his privileges and status within specific communities, Paul does not mention Roman citizenship.[32]

For example, in his second letter to the Corinthians, Paul boasts of his achievements and the honored status he held before encountering Christ, but he does not include citizenship (2 Cor. 11:22–29). When he writes his letter to the Philippians, a community who had known him since the very beginning of his ministry, Paul lists all of the honors and privileges he gave up for Christ, including his circumcision, his perfect fulfillment of Torah, and his status as a Jewish teacher, a speaker of

Hebrew, and a persecutor of the church (Phil. 3:4–11), but he does not mention Roman citizenship.[33] Paul also wrote to the Philippian churches from prison, a context that might give rise to putting one's hope in one's citizenship status as a get-out-of-jail card. But Paul wrote that he did not know how long he would be incarcerated. He could only "trust in the Lord" that he would see the Philippian churches again soon (2:23–24). Paul took comfort in his chains not because he could appeal to the emperor for a fair trial but because he had the Philippians' support and the help of Christ's Spirit (1:7–14).

In all of his letters, Paul only mentions "citizenship" twice (Phil. 1:27; 3:20).[34] In Philippians 1:27 Paul refers to "being citizens of the gospel of Christ" (my translation). This is not membership in an earthly government with special privileges over other people who are not members; it is a "citizenship in heaven" (Phil. 3:20). Membership in God's kingdom, Christ's (political) body, is inclusive and comes not from the emperor's favor but from sharing in Christ's humility (2:1–8). Thus it appears that Paul, like Hugo, had to wait in jail for the legal process to unfold, rather than appeal to the privilege of citizenship to save him (2:23–24).

Humiliation, Suffering, and Loss of Status

In addition to expulsion from cities and lack of citizenship, Paul also suffers the same humiliation and loss of status in prison that Hugo does in detention. In his letters, Paul reports that he was accused and arrested many times (2 Cor. 11:23–25). But the greatest charge against Paul came later in his life. Christian tradition holds that the Roman Empire charged Paul with challenging the emperor's sovereignty and defaming the imperial name. Ultimately, later Christian bishops reported that Paul was executed for his crimes against the emperor in Rome in 64 CE.[35]

Prior to his execution, we do not know for sure how long Paul was in prison or what type of incarceration he experienced.[36] Frankly, none of the options for incarceration for a man of Paul's modest means were desirable or even remotely tolerable. Prisoners awaiting trial could be thrown in a pit or a cave packed with other prisoners; they could be chained to a guard and held in confinement; or they could be kept under house arrest in their own home, if they had one, or in the home of a patron. In his letter to the Philippians, Paul describes being "chained" and under guard as he awaits trial (Phil. 1:12–14). He does not comment on the charges, except to intimate that his conviction might end in execution (1:20–24).[37]

If Paul was chained to a prison guard and detained that way until his hearing,[38] we can reconstruct a bit more detail about his circumstances. All of a prisoner's actions were under the guard's scrutiny. Prisoners in chains were at the mercy of their guard to move, eat, drink, relieve themselves, sleep, and even to speak to visitors or to dictate letters to an associate. A prisoner chained to a guard could do nothing without the guard's permission; he was, essentially, enslaved to the whims and movements of a Roman official. The experience of multiple imprisonments is one likely source for Paul's suffering "weaknesses, insults, hardships, and calamities for the sake of Christ" (2 Cor. 12:10).[39]

Comparing Hugo's and Paul's Stories

To be sure, the circumstances and details of Hugo's and Paul's incarcerations are different. Paul was arrested for disturbing the peace and speaking against the gods—both crimes against the Roman social order. He also could have been prosecuted for treason for insulting the emperor.[40] Hugo was detained for his immigration status and for reentering the country illegally after being deported the first time. But it is reasonable to think that

Paul's and Hugo's fear, humiliation, and loss of status—and perhaps even their lack of citizenship—are similar. Both men are chained, body and hands. Both men must submit to the direction of guards and are dependent on someone else to provide food, water, bed, clothing, bathroom services, and even physical activities. They are not permitted to earn a living, organize their own time, receive gifts without permission, or determine their daily activities. They can have visitors, following the institutional regulations, if permitted by the guards. They can write letters, if they purchase the necessary equipment. Neither man receives a timeline for his legal process, a release date, or relief from the basic physical suffering of hunger, boredom, restricted movement, and isolation from their loved ones.

Additionally, the social stigma that Paul and Hugo experience in prison can quickly extend to their family and friends. Hugo worries about how others will perceive him and his family. "I want them to know we are good people," he writes.[41] Paul may desire the same, but many preachers and opponents are taking advantage of his arrest. Some are simply wary of him, while others publicly pull their support from him or start campaigns against him, "intending to increase my suffering in my imprisonment" (Phil. 1:17). One of the reasons Paul writes to the Philippian congregations is to reassure them that he remains committed to their shared mission. His arrest will not derail their work in Christ (1:12). Still, he acknowledges and thanks them for their solidarity with him while he is in prison (1:3–7). He prays for them, gives thanks for their shared energies, resources, and support, "both in my imprisonment and in the defense and confirmation of the gospel" (1:7).

A key hardship for both Paul and Hugo is the financial burden their loved ones bear while they are in prison. Both men are proud of their labor and the work they have done with their own hands. They prefer not to burden the very people for whom they have worked so hard to provide. Paul reminds his churches in a letter to "remember our labor and toil, brothers and sisters; we worked night and day, so that we might not burden any of you. . . . You are witnesses, and God also, how pure, upright, and blameless our conduct was toward you" (1 Thess. 2:9–10; see also 1 Cor. 4:12). Hugo writes, "I paid my taxes and I worked hard to support my family."[42] In their letters, Paul and Hugo report not having enough to eat, but they are not worried for themselves. They are worried for their loved ones. For Hugo, this means a deep anxiety about the financial impact his incarceration has on his wife and children. For Paul, this means not taking advantage of the Philippians' financial assistance. Still, he has to acknowledge his deep appreciation for the money they sent with one of their members, Epaphroditus (Phil. 4:18). Paul thanks them for sending other supplies as well—perhaps a coat, a blanket, or food, all of which would have to be shared with the guard at the other end of his chains. Paul gives thanks to God for the Philippians' solidarity and asks God to repay their financial support of his preaching ministry and of Paul himself (4:15–20).

Paul and Hugo are grateful for visitors. Hugo looks forward to his children's visit every couple of weeks, and he keeps daily contact with his wife by pay phone. Without a phone system or car to cover the distance quickly, Paul is dependent on his longtime associate in ministry, Timothy, to relay messages to his churches on foot. Timothy can move freely, bringing news to Paul from the outside world, friends, associates, and churches (Phil. 2:19; 1 Thess. 3:6). He also takes news and carries letters from Paul to Paul's supporters (1 Cor. 4:17; Phil. 2:19; 1 Thess. 3:1–2). Meanwhile, the Philippian churches send their associate, Epaphroditus, to visit Paul, to provide a few supplies, and to convey their concern and encouragement (Phil. 4:15–18). When he returns to Philippi, Epaphroditus carries the New Testament letter we call Philippians, likely after review and approval by the prison guard (2:25–28). Because he visited Paul in person,

Epaphroditus also carries unwritten news of Paul's welfare, his emotional state, the prison conditions, and any available updates on the legal procedures. In between these visits, the house-church networks across the Roman Empire move news back and forth between Paul and his associates, supporters, and loved ones (1 Cor. 1:11). In the US, faith-based and not-for-profit advocacy groups as well as churches create similar networks, sharing messages about detainees' welfare with their families and supporters. They also coordinate care for detained immigrants, getting the word out about abuses and lack of food in detention centers.

This all sounds routine. But during personal visits and in the exchange of letters and care packages, there is always the danger that friends of the incarcerated or the detained might come under suspicion or incriminate themselves. Paul feared that some from his congregations would leave Christ when they experienced persecutions like he did (1 Thess. 3:3). It is also possible that some in his churches distanced themselves from Paul because his reputation could negatively affect their social status (2 Cor. 10:10). Paul's Roman guard could decide that Timothy was an accomplice to Paul's work and arrest Timothy as well.[43]

Detainees in the US share this fear. Hugo's eldest children each had a legal reprieve from deportation through their DACA (Deferred Action for Childhood Arrivals) status, but the reprieve was temporary. By frequently visiting their father in detention, might Hugo's children aggravate their prospects for renewing their permission to stay in the US? Hugo's un-documented wife was also at risk because of her husband's case, all the more so when their family decided to publicize Hugo's story. The possibility of further arrests or detentions adds to the emotional strain Paul and Hugo experience. The last thing they want is to draw their loved ones into their legal processes.

In 64 CE, there was an end to Paul's repeated arrests and incarcerations. Christian tradition reports that Paul was executed in Rome for crimes against the emperor. Paul's preaching that Christ is Lord, particularly as a stranger in cities where he had no local network, could easily become a charge of treason against the imperial head of state, the divine emperor. From Paul's letter to the Philippians, it seems Paul did not know whether he would be released or whether he would be executed (Phil. 1:20). And still he held out hope, telling them, "I will come to you again" (Phil. 2:24).

When Hugo wrote his story online, he too did not know the outcome of his detention. Immigration detention would not end in execution, but it could quickly end Hugo's life in America. And, if Hugo and his wife kept their family together, deportation would end the American lives of all of his children, even of the youngest, the US citizen.

Thankfully, Hugo was released from detention on bond in 2017, just before Thanksgiving.[44] He had been in detention for over six months. In Hugo's case, the strength of support from his community, his union, his family, and others made a difference in his outcome. The other man who had been picked up with Hugo by ICE had been immediately deported.

Theological Reflections for Christian Practice

Hugo addresses us—the American people living in the US. Paul addresses his first-century churches—and Christians believe he addresses us today. After observing the similarities between Hugo's detention and Paul's incarceration, we can learn from Paul's theological reflections on the role of the Philippian Christians in responding to his imprisonment. How Paul addresses these first-century Christians can help American Christians today think about the role we should play in responding to the detention of immigrants like Hugo.

Sharing in Joy and Suffering

In his letter to the Philippians, Paul first gives thanks for their *koinōnia* (participation and sharing) with him while he is incarcerated. They had been constant in their support, sharing in his distress (Phil. 4:14) even when they were unable to be with him in person (2:29–30) or to help him financially (4:10). He writes, "It is right for me to think this way about all of you, because you hold me in your heart, for all of you share in God's grace with me, both in my imprisonment and in the defense and confirmation of the gospel" (1:7). Paul rejoices when the Philippians are finally able to help him again financially (4:10, 14). He praises their *koinōnia* again—their sharing his trouble by sending help—especially when no one else was there to assist him (4:15). He acknowledges that they sent help "more than once" (4:16).

Paul recognizes that the Philippians are partners (*koinōnoi*) with him in God's grace. They not only share in Christ's gospel; they also stand with him in prison. They have prayed for Paul, as he prays for them, and Paul believes that their prayers, with Christ's help, will result in his release (1:19). Their *koinōnia* with him (2:17–18) makes all the difference in Paul's own ability to face difficult circumstances (1:20–26, 29–30).

Hugo and other immigrants are asking for this same consideration—*koinōnia*, a shared humanity. When we recognize the humanity of people in detention, then we can advocate for their humane treatment. We can share their joy and suffering as fellow human beings; as Christians, we can pray for them, honor their stories, and offer our compassion. When we recognize our shared desires for our families, our shared love of neighbor, and our shared need for safety, health, home, and opportunities, then we are practicing what Paul calls "the mind of Christ" (2:1–5).

Serving Our Neighbor and Making an Offering to God

Another point Paul makes in his letter to the Philippians is that serving our neighbor is making a worshipful offering to God. Paul tells the Philippians, "I have been paid in full and have more than enough; I am fully satisfied, now that I have received from Epaphroditus the gifts you sent, a fragrant offering, a sacrifice acceptable and pleasing to God" (Phil. 4:18). For Paul, the prayers, support, love, ministry, and financial help the Philippians send to him in prison through Epaphroditus are not, ultimately, for him. In the very same sentence, Paul shifts from the financial language of gifts between friends to the religious language of making an offering of service and worship to God.[45] In other words, the Philippians' *koinōnia*, the love and gifts and fellowship they share with Paul in prison, *is* their offering to God.

When we begin with love of neighbor, or, as the Philippians did, when we begin by cultivating humility and love as disciples of Christ, learning about our immigrant neighbors and hearing their stories is an easy step. Letting that love of Christ "overflow more and more with knowledge" (Phil. 1:9) can grow into actions of support for our neighbors, even *koinōnia*—sharing in the circumstances—with our detained brothers and sisters. Just as the Philippians prayed for and supported Paul—sending letters, gifts, and Epaphroditus to him in prison—we can do the same for those detained like Hugo. This is, in Paul's thinking, "a fragrant offering, a sacrifice acceptable and pleasing to God" (4:18).

Love That Overflows in Knowledge

Paul reminds the Philippians that their knowledge, like his, is limited. He urges humility (2:3), and he prays for their love to grow so that they may come to "full insight" and experience the kind of love that overflows "with knowledge" and discernment

(1:9–10). For Paul, love comes *before* complete knowledge, and when one loves more, more knowledge comes. This is critical for Christians to remember today. "We know only in part" (1 Cor. 13:9, 12). Rather than argue with only partial knowledge and limited understanding of complex immigration issues, and rather than judge people before we hear their stories, we are called to practice love, compassion, and humility (2:1–5). Paul tells the Philippians to lead with humility and love so that when their knowledge grows, then they might determine "what is best" (1:9–10).

American citizens all need more knowledge of immigration issues because we are all responsible for the safe treatment, physical health, and psychological welfare of those we detain while they seek legal status among us. After all, we set up these immigration laws, and we live within the borders these laws protect. We pay the GEO Group and other for-profit corporations to run deportation centers, using our tax dollars to house, feed, clothe, and keep men, women, and children safe in a contained and strictly regulated environment. We need to begin to educate ourselves about US legal policies and procedures. We must become familiar with the effects these policies and procedures have on the people who are subject to them.

Putting Love and Knowledge into Practice

First, we can learn the facts about who is affected by our immigration and detention policies so that we can offer support to vulnerable people as they move through the legal processes. One way to do this is to read the online stories of the individual people we maintain in our detention system. You can read these letters and stories from detainees posted on the IMM-Print website, a storytelling project hosted by Freedom for Immigrants.[46] These stories, letters, art pieces, and short bios are not news clips sensationalized for prime time. They are not touched up or edited for a specific political audience. They are simply the words of detainees who wish to tell us their stories in an open and public forum. While each voice and story is unique, most of the detained writers testify to feeling an acute anxiety for their families and a deep desire to live in America and contribute to the American dream.

I am not advocating here for open borders. I agree with Robert Frost that "good fences make good neighbors." I also agree with most Americans that we need clear and just immigration policies in the US and that we need to enforce them.[47] But our immigration policies have not been clear or just for decades. Our policies do not meet basic ethical standards in the treatment of the people who cross borders or the people we have detained inside our borders as they move through the legal immigration processes. Even on this side of the "wall," immigrants are still our neighbors. And, more importantly, they are vulnerable. Once they cross US borders without permission, these immigrant neighbors do not have rights under our US Constitution, and they therefore require extra care, protection from institutional abuses, and repeated witness to their humanity.

Violating US immigration law is a civil, not a federal, offense. For this civil offense, there is no statute of limitations for prosecution.[48] This means we detain undocumented immigrants in the US regardless of how long they have lived and worked among us and regardless of how or why they came. As Christians, those of us who have the rights of citizens and residents also have the responsibility to listen compassionately to our undocumented neighbors, especially those who have risked everything to live side by side with us and have contributed positively to our neighborhoods and faith communities. As Christians, we have the responsibility to respond compassionately to those in detention, to be attentive to the wrenching emotional and financial toll that the legal process

takes on their families, and to consider the detrimental economic impact their long-term detainment has on our court systems and federal resources. We must also consider the simple,
straightforward witness of Scripture: "Love your neighbor as
yourself" (Matt. 22:39). Christ calls us to walk with our most
vulnerable neighbors—those who do not have the protections
of legal status in our country.

Second, we can get involved by visiting detainees or hearing
from others who make these visits. Churches and other faith-
based organizations can sponsor volunteers to visit those who
are isolated in detention centers across the nation. Detention
Witness is an organization that trains volunteers to accompany
those who are detained while in the process of applying for a
legal way to stay in the US.[49] Volunteers working with groups
like Detention Witness are particularly important for the encouragement of detainees who do not have family members
who can visit them. Detention Witness volunteers support our
immigrant neighbors in detention by simply offering their presence, bringing personal messages of hope and encouragement,
and providing a connection to the outside. Once you have seen
the effect of detention center conditions on the heart and psyche
of another human being, it is difficult to turn your back. You
want to tell their story. Detention Witness ambassadors visit
detainees, and they return to their faith communities to educate
their fellow citizens about the plight of the most vulnerable
in our US detention systems. Like Timothy did for Paul (Phil.
2:19–24), such volunteers carry the voice of the detainees into
the open and share them with a wider audience.

If we can't volunteer to visit detainees, we can sponsor others
to visit and share their stories. The Philippian churches sponsored one of their own, Epaphroditus, to visit Paul in prison,
carry supplies to him, and return to them with news (Phil.
2:25–30; 4:14–18). When Epaphroditus arrived in Philippi carrying Paul's letter as well as news and greetings, the community

would have gathered to hear the letter and to receive updates on the legal proceedings.[50] Then they prepared to receive Timothy, Paul's associate who was with Paul in prison and would bring news of the verdict in Paul's case at a later date (Phil. 2:23). Likewise, local congregations, Hugo's union, and others in the community surrounded his children and his wife to help with gas, food bills, encouragement, and legal costs. Today these basic levels of compassion, support, and self-education are something all congregations can do proactively to support detainees.

Third, there is also the work of advocacy. This is the work of groups like Freedom for Immigrants, Al Otro Lado, the Matthew 25 / Mateo 25 movement, and The Young Center for Immigrant Children's Rights.[51] Freedom for Immigrants is a national organization that works to end immigrant detention. Toward that goal, they created an Immigrant Legal Resource Center to consult on and advocate for policies that have made detention center conditions more humane. For example, they have cosponsored legislation for the right to in-person (rather than video) visitation, the right to reasonable phone call rates, and the right to detention inspection by third-party groups. Al Otro Lado ("on the other side") focuses on refugee and immigrant needs on the border between the US and Mexico. Begun in 2012, this project offers direct legal advocacy, family reunification, and employment for migrants, immigrants, and refugees on both sides of the border. In addition to legal advocacy, they also organize weeklong volunteer projects at the border. The Matthew 25 / Mateo 25 movement began in 2016 in Southern California by inviting Christians to take a pledge "to stand with and defend the vulnerable in the name of Jesus."[52] Their advocacy begins with prayer, education, and identifying local community resources that can be mobilized on behalf of the vulnerable. The Young Center for Immigrant Children's Rights recruits and trains volunteers to accompany immigrant children through the legal process.[53] These advocacy groups are working to hold our American institutions to the highest standards of our justice system and of our moral commitments as a society.

Finally, there is theological work to be done. Many Christian scholars are at work on behalf of immigrant and undocumented neighbors. I am adding my voice to their work.[54] You too can read the Scriptures through the eyes of those who are more vulnerable than you. You can also testify to other Christians using the stories of border crossing in our Scriptures. Help other Christians see the parallels between Paul's experiences and those of a construction worker named Hugo, or those of other border crossers who witness to Christ in our midst. Paul invites the Philippians to see the vulnerability of Christ in his own first-century chains (Phil. 1:13). I invite you to see the vulnerability of Christ in the stories of those who cross borders today, in the suffering of those who are separated from their families as they await legal hearings in detention centers across the US, and in the solidarity of those who stand with immigrant detainees and their families.

Paul argues that, by standing together to support him in his incarceration, and by striving together to be citizens of Christ rather than of the empire, the Philippians are embodying the mind of Christ (Phil. 2:1–11). Further, by welcoming Timothy and Epaphroditus in their vulnerability and ministry with Paul, the Philippians open themselves up to experience Christ's vulnerability and humility.[55] With Paul in ancient times, the Philippians risk their privilege, status, and well-being. They receive Timothy and Epaphroditus with open arms and hospitality, as if Christ were walking into their congregational meeting (2:28–30). And they prepare to receive Paul—a man with a mixed reputation, fresh out of prison, if he is indeed released from prison (1:19; 2:23–30). In these acts, Paul reasons, the Philippians are working out their salvation as God is at work in them (Phil. 2:12–13).

Our Citizenship Is in Heaven

Today Paul reminds us, just as he reminded the Philippians, that although some of us are privileged to have citizenship in the countries where we live, what is most valuable is our shared citizenship in heaven (Phil. 3:20). This heavenly citizenship is ours in Christ (3:20); it does not come from a US passport. Citizenship in Christ is not lost when DACA runs out, nor is it threatened when national policies change. What changes with immigration law, policy, and the implementation of these as borders between neighbors is our "human form"—it is how we administrate national borders. With respect to Christ, we all have the same citizenship; to embody this citizenship in the body of Christ is our heavenly calling.

We live out our heavenly calling by standing with those who are made vulnerable by their loss of status: prisoners, detainees, those who prioritize the good of others, and those who risk harm to themselves, and even death, to serve their community. We exercise our heavenly citizenship by imitating Paul, who imitated Christ, accepting a vulnerable social status. It is when we experience that social vulnerability and cross those status boundaries, leaving our comfort zones and stepping out of our privileged social locations, that we begin to know Christ and his power as Paul did—not the power of our own resources, political affiliations, earnings, and gains, but the power of his resurrection and cosmic glory that God offers to the most vulnerable among us.

Will we cling to our status and privileges as US citizens, while others have no protections? Or will we stand with our vulnerable border-crossing neighbors who do not share our privileges of birth, education, resources, and political stability? As Americans, will we buy into the lie that the more people who cross the border to share the American dream, the weaker the dream becomes? Afraid that our privileges will be diluted, will we try to hang on to those privileges by keeping others out—keeping would-be immigrants out with border walls or containing border crossers in detention centers? Or will we cling to what is simply a gift, a heavenly citizenship that we live into precisely by showing compassion to our immigrant and detainee brothers and sisters, hearing their stories, learning about the struggles they face, and advocating on their behalf, knowing that their presence makes our communities and our nation not weaker but stronger?

6

Seeking Asylum at the US Border

Philippians 2:5–11

US Detention Centers: Documented Conditions behind the Walls

It was December 2017 when I drove a few hours into the California desert to meet Jorge and James. It was my first visit with ICE detainees at the Adelanto Detention Center in Victorville. Adelanto is a federal immigration facility run by the private, for-profit corporation GEO Group.[1] Adelanto is also the largest detention center in California, with capacity for two thousand detainees.[2] For many of these detainees, as for James, arriving at Adelanto means the end of their American dream. Here, detainees find themselves in a no-man's-land, a holding cage for unauthorized immigrants who were wandering in the California desert, were pulled off the streets of a US town, or who turned themselves in at the border to seek asylum.

By definition, a detention center is not a prison because it does not impose punishment. But GEO Group runs both prisons and detention centers on the same physical campus, and often the detention center is simply a repurposed prison building. Typically, people detained for immigration violations or held for asylum hearings ("detainees") are housed in cells in detention centers until they appear before an immigration court to be found innocent or guilty of civil, not criminal, penalties.[3] To a detainee, life looks and feels like prison life. They give up all personal belongings, wear mandated uniforms, follow the institutional schedule, eat the institutional food, and need permission from the guards to use the pay phone, common room, showers, printers, mail, and to receive visitors. Any of these "privileges" can be revoked for even a small infraction.

Like many Americans, I had assumed that detainees were people who had committed a crime—that they had been picked up for living in the US without documentation or had crossed the border illegally. The reality is quite different. From Jorge and James I learned that many people are seeking asylum. They make incredible, and often long and harrowing, journeys to the US border to request asylum as permitted by US law.[4]

Gaining legal entry into the US is usually very difficult, and no matter which route one takes, it is almost always a long process. A US visa provides temporary resident status under almost endless, carefully defined categories,[5] while a green card provides permanent residency status but not citizenship. Even under normal circumstances, legal entry for refugees is not straightforward, affordable, or rational. There aren't clear steps to follow. There are financial costs, changing federal quotas by country, lotteries, shifting standards of entry, and, except in a few circumstances, years of waiting.[6] Legal entry to the US requires exquisite timing, a significant amount of money, an extreme tolerance for ambiguity, or all of the above. But when people's lives are in danger or the lives of their children are threatened, they will take incredible risks to make it to the US border.

Those who arrive at the border and request asylum are often poor, and many are desperate, but they have not committed a crime. Asylum seekers submit to the border patrol procedures. They are often separated from children, spouses, or other family members who travel with them. They endure institutional humiliations, overworked border officials, overcrowded intake facilities, and in some cases, inhumane conditions. From that point, ICE takes them into custody and moves them to a detention center.

Like prisons, detention centers house individuals by gender. They cannot accommodate families who arrive together—a parent and a child, a husband and a wife, or a brother and a sister. In the center I visited, detainees described their living conditions like this. An adult male typically lives in a cell with five other men, sleeps in a bunk, and uses the stainless-steel sink and toilet—without a stall—during the day. There is no privacy. He has access to the public shower with a group of men for a set day and time. Communal meals are tightly scheduled, as are short windows of time to access the public television, pay phone, or an outdoor courtyard that may be crowded. Detainees can choose to work in the laundry, kitchen, or janitorial detail for one dollar a day. That money goes into personal accounts that detainees can use at the "convenience store" for cigarettes, stamps, paper, pens, and nonperishable food items (Cup Noodles is a popular choice) for twice the amount that you or I might pay.

When I looked into the institutional side of detention centers, I started with the Department of Homeland Security website. According to their November 2017 statistics, for-profit companies run 71 percent of US detention centers. These centers, many of them juvenile detention centers, house detainees who are considered "not a threat." The contracted standards of care for detention centers are not uniform across the detention system. Some centers follow American Correctional Association accreditation guidelines—that is, penal guidelines, even though detention is not punitive.[7] How can we house noncriminal asylum seekers in US institutions built for criminal offenders and managed by for-profit companies—that is, companies that have a financial interest in seeing more people detained, for longer periods of time, and housed more cheaply? And, given this situation, why would anyone come to the border and submit to this process?

Understanding the complexity of the myriad situations and circumstances that have brought people to our US immigrant detention centers requires more than one chapter in a book. Political issues, economic issues, mental and psychological issues, family issues, and the global market are all at play and demand careful attention. Detention centers and their staff do not distinguish between legal asylum seekers and people who have been living in the US without permission. All must await their turn before an immigration judge in court. It is important to consider their stories and the conditions we, as taxpayers and voters, ask immigrants to submit to while they wait.

Visiting Adelanto Detention Center

When I first visited Adelanto Detention Center, I accompanied a coordinator from Detention Witness, a program organized through Clergy and Laity United for Economic Justice in Ventura County (CLUE-VC) working in partnership with Freedom for Immigrants.[8] Both organizations are not-for-profit immigrant advocacy groups. Freedom for Immigrants works to end the isolation detainees experience in detention by advocating for their release into a supportive community while they follow the legal process.[9]

Visiting a detention center is relatively easy for citizens. We parked, walked across the parking lot into the compound, made our visits, and hours later returned to the car with little discomfort. But I also know that behind these walls and fences covered in razor wire, beyond the sterile halls that are open to the public, there are cells controlled by mechanical doors that lock with people inside. Yet they say this is not a prison.

We entered through the front door. Uniformed officers came and went through the same door. We walked into a large waiting room. Rows of chairs lined either side of an aisle that led to an open counter with guards who were processing visitor IDs. We got in line, standing a few feet back from the counter to wait our turn like one does at the pharmacy—to give a little privacy, space, or security distance to the people at the counter. When it was my turn, I signed in at the desk, gave the "a" number of the detainee I wished to visit, and left my driver's license with the guard (I later learned that "a" stood for "alien"). She gave me a key for a locker in which to leave my purse, phone, watch, and jacket. We could carry nothing into the visitation room with us. I tried to imagine visiting a spouse or parent without a valid driver's license. The visitor system seemed to be designed for people who have documentation.

In the Waiting Room

Once signed in, we sat in the rows of chairs and waited. I watched family members, friends, priests, lawyers, and other advocates enter and exit during the visiting hours. The only inconvenience was a long wait. The more experienced volunteers for Detention Witness told us that the visitation allowance is one hour and that they try to group people to enter at the same time. Depending on how many visitors are waiting, we could be in the next group, or we might have to wait an hour or two to enter with a subsequent group of visitors.

I watched children play tag and toddlers wobble across shiny institutional floors with older siblings or grandparents just two steps behind. Many families were dressed up for the occasion: little girls wore frilly dresses and ladies wore lipstick and heels. Teenagers slouched in their chairs, whether bored or hypnotized by the small screen in their hands is hard to say. Women chatted about everything. Older men traded stories, mostly in Spanish. We camped out together, amicably, in the plastic chairs. It felt almost mundane. I was new to this space between "inside" and "outside," but most people in the waiting room were making their weekly or monthly pilgrimage to visit a loved one.

Two or three rounds of visitors entered ahead of us in large groups to meet dads, brothers, sons, or husbands. I was there to meet strangers whom Detention Witness had asked us to visit. While many had been detained in the US and had local networks or family members within a one-hundred-mile radius, the men we visited had no family in the US. They were mentally languishing in isolation from friends, family, and community. They suffered from anxiety arising out of the ambiguity of their legal status and the inadequate physical conditions. They tried to hold themselves together mentally and emotionally, and they would tell fellow detainees about us. Requests for visits from the Detention Witness "friends" continued to grow.

Isolation behind the Walls

It is easy for those of us on the outside to underestimate the isolation and desolation people experience when they are locked behind these walls. The toll was visible in people's faces. After just one visit I could see the stress eating these men alive. There are always more requests for visits than Detention Witness can serve, and they are looking for more volunteers. Our leader explained that the work is pretty simple: to offer human support while the men (and the women housed in another building) wait in legal limbo. We listen to the detainee, ask questions, share stories, and offer encouragement. After the visit, we make note of the conditions they describe and document any abuses or concerns they report so that Detention Witness can advocate for them. It's important to share with the person we visit that Americans outside the detention center walls care about them, are praying for them, and are working through our legal system to advocate for a safe, quick, and just process for every legal case. "Remember," our leader said, "we are not here to subvert or circumscribe the existing legal process. We are here to walk with people during their immigration process so that their experience behind the border of these detention center walls is more humane."

The Work of Visiting Volunteers

On the drive home, our leader shared her experience that these visits can be hopeful as well as emotionally difficult. Over the long term, immigrant advocacy and accompaniment can be grim, disheartening work. In the process you learn that many state courts are booked solid for years from the date of an individual's detention. Detainees find it all but impossible to gather the evidence they need to support their asylum case. With no Internet access, limited access to pay-per-use phones, and no cash for long-distance or international calls, they can't get the documents they need. If they can hire or find a lawyer to work with, even that person on the outside has difficulties obtaining documentation in support of an asylum case. Detainees leave their home countries precisely because those countries lack the government and institutional infrastructures to maintain a civilian police force, let alone to maintain public records. Countries facing war, famine, political upheaval, or widespread poverty do not prioritize record keeping. When people flee, they do not stop to pick up the threatening note, the medical records of broken bones, the photos documenting abuse, or the recorded testimony of witnesses. Obtaining the evidence required for asylum, or even obtaining birth and marriage records to prove place of origin, is frustrating and often impossible. Even with the necessary documentation to prove threat of life, the US detention appeal process and the asylum request process, like our legal immigration process, are complex, restrictive, and time-consuming to navigate.

However well-intentioned we may be in volunteering to visit a detainee, it is awkward to sit for the first time with a complete stranger inside the detention center. Some visits happen in the communal visitation room, face-to-face in small plastic chairs around low tables, close enough to hear the people at the table next to you. At other times you must speak to the person through thick glass using a telephone receiver. This is for their safety, not yours. In both situations, conversation can feel forced. There are lulls, silences, even nervous laughter. Sometimes conversation is limited because of language barriers or personalities. The point is simply to be there.

As a newcomer, I was most aware of all that I could not do. Pencils and paper are not allowed. Visitors and detainees may not exchange anything—not even a scrap of paper—unless the guard provides it. In my own nervousness, I wanted to offer something, mostly to ground myself. I reached for the role of the host to feel some kind of control over this strange context. I longed for all the things a host might offer to ease the awkwardness: a cup of tea, freshly baked bread, a family photo, a comic book, or news about loved ones my conversation partner must be desperate to hear. Of course, playing host made no sense at all. And I knew that I was making assumptions about who these detainees were and what they missed and longed for. I knew that I had no idea what detention was truly like for the men and women we sat down to visit.

Jorge's Story

During this first visit to Adelanto Detention Center I met a young man, recently arrived, whom I'll call Jorge. Jorge had lived in a border town in Mexico. His father was a security guard for a local business. He had a younger sister at home. One day Jorge approached the US border guards and asked for asylum. In speaking with me he was circumspect about the details that led him to the decision to turn himself in. But as we spoke I gathered that he had been pressured by local drug lords from a young age. His family could not protect him, and finally the cartel pulled him out of school, forcing him into illicit work. When he could no longer tolerate the cartel, he turned himself in for protection. He was sixteen.

The border patrol handed Jorge over to ICE officers who placed him in a juvenile detention center for fifteen months. Jorge was OK with that—in juvenile detention he could attend classes with other teens. In quiet Spanish he told me that it "wasn't great, but it was good. I could study. I was still in the *secundaria*. I want to study, and I want to graduate. In juvenile detention I studied and I worked. They moved us around a lot. Nine months there, six weeks there, three months somewhere else . . ."

On his eighteenth birthday, ICE moved Jorge to the detention center in Adelanto. A teenager landed in an adult world. Here, among the men, Jorge kept to his cell for safety. I asked him if there was room to exercise. Not really. He told me they were allowed to leave their cell and go out into "the yard." But, he said, his eyes inching sideways, "it's crowded out there, and dangerous. In the yard, you have to be careful where you walk. It's better to stay inside." His words were chilling. In crowded gathering places like the exercise yard, Jorge was an easy target for men picking fights or recruiting for gangs.

From Jorge I learned that detention centers' systems and protocols are similar to institutional prisons. Detainees wear color-coded clothes that communicate whether or not they have a past criminal record, and, if they do, what kind of conviction they served time for. Jorge, like the older men in his cell, wore dark blue scrubs indicating no past criminal record. He could be in the same room with men wearing orange scrubs indicating they had, at some point in their life, committed a nonviolent crime such as a drug offense. The men in orange had paid their fine, or served their time, and were now held at Adelanto for an immigration violation. In fact, "by law, immigration detention must be civil in nature, not punitive."[10]

There was a third group of men dressed in red scrubs. The men wearing red had, at one time in their life, been convicted of a more serious or violent crime. Like the men in orange, the men in red had also served their time and were now detained solely on an immigration violation. Even so, men in blue scrubs could not be in the same room as men in red scrubs. With respect to the law, none of the detainees were inmates or serving time. They were all waiting to put their civil case before an immigration judge. Yet they were color coded and wore their past records on their bodies.

Because of the color codes, I had to meet Jorge in a "noncontact" room—basically a small room with thick glass walls and telephones on each side of the glass. It took some explanation to understand why we had to talk by telephone. At the time, the guard explained, the visitation room was full of men wearing red. Jorge could not be in that visitation room since he wore blue. So I could either wait an hour for the visitation room to clear, or I could meet Jorge in the small noncontact room, where he would be isolated from the men in red. The color codes were procedurally logical. However, in practice they made little sense. To get to the telephone room I walked through the open visitation room full of men in red, yet Jorge could not sit there with me while the men in red were present. As I passed through the room, the men in red were chatting with their families and hugging their daughters, sons, wives, and brothers.

When I asked him about the color codes, Jorge explained that he could mix with men in blue and men in orange (*azules y anaranjados*), but not with the men in red (*los arojados*) fill-ing the visitation room behind me. As a civilian, I did not need protection; these men in red were just like anyone else I might have passed on a public street. But here, everyone's past was vis-ible. This is partly why Jorge chose to remain in his cell during the day. Men in blue could get hurt being in the wrong place at the wrong time. Later, I heard from other volunteers that teen-agers were easy targets for gang recruitment and, sometimes, sexual assault. The color codes were an institutional attempt to protect men from one another inside the detention center.

Jorge was shy and soft-spoken. It was hard to hear him over the crackling phone line. Still, after tolerating my opening awk-ward questions, he looked me in the eyes: "I've been here a month. They don't feed us enough—that's why everyone here is so skinny! You can buy more food—but it's twice the price of food outside. They mark everything up. I have some money saved up from when I worked in the juvenile detention centers. But I don't want to leave my cell to work here."

I was able to confirm that the institutional services provided in detention centers by for-profit groups like GEO Group are less than adequate. Centers are required to provide three meals a day, health care, three sets of scrubs (of blue, orange, or red), and little else. Jorge told me someone had stolen a set of his scrubs, and now he only had what he was wearing and the set that was in the laundry. He told me that the running joke among the detainees was that the skinnier you were, the longer you had been there. Everyone goes hungry, he said. Dinner might be peanut butter and jelly. Lunch might be broth.

While Jorge was carefully groomed and his manner was guarded, I met other detainees who were visibly agitated, re-ported trouble sleeping, and were anxious, depressed, and worried—about their own cases, their families, their future. Like Jorge, these asylum seekers were not serving time for a criminal conviction. They were simply awaiting an immigration hearing before a judge. I learned that many detainees cannot endure the conditions long enough to move through the six-to-twelve-month legal process—they self-deport. But even self-deportation, once the papers are signed, can take weeks to a month to process. For these and many other reasons, for-profit detention centers like Adelanto receive heavy criticism from immigrant advocates and international human rights groups.[11]

As we neared the end of our hour-long visit, I had to ask Jorge why he agreed to meet with me, a complete stranger. His answer was unexpected: "It's something to do." I had come with good intentions and a desire to convey support from Americans outside. But for Jorge, the visit was just a diversion. I flashed back to the teenagers I had seen in the waiting room—glued to their cell phones, linked to the world, and consuming whatever the Internet was serving up. Jorge's world was a cell he shared with five men, and a group TV room. Finally, I understood. The boy was bored out of his mind. His curiosity had no outlet; his body had no exercise; his mind had nothing to explore or learn or reflect on. He had no diversions from the unrelenting institutional rhythm that shaped his life. Without Internet, a phone, friends, cousins, siblings, or parents, without school, games, or a neighborhood, what was there to do? No wonder he agreed to meet a random visitor. I provided a break in the routine.

As a college professor, I teach eighteen-year-olds day in and day out for fifteen weeks at a time. They are curious, respectful, and impish, part adult and part child, struggling and striving, learning, dreaming, creating, exploring, and testing limits and overcoming them. They are full of energy, passion, angst, rebel-lion, fearlessness, and trepidation—all in one human bundle of dynamic possibility. In Jorge's case, I could not imagine what the blank walls, restricted socializing, limited nutrition, and lack of physical exercise were doing to this eighteen-year-old. Fifteen months ago, he had turned himself in at the US border seeking protection from the mafia bosses he refused to work for. He simply wanted to go to school. Our sixty-minute halting conversation left me feeling embarrassed by my own lofty desire to help. That desire seemed so small, inadequate, and, frankly, bizarre alongside the shape of Jorge's daily reality and the real vulnerability of his status in our world.

When I got up to leave the visitation room, my first visit was over. After one more visit and a long drive I would arrive home, change clothes, unwind, and share a meal with my family. When the eighteen-year-old sitting opposite me got up, he left the no-contact room in the same blue scrubs he would wake up in tomorrow. He filed out of his glass enclosure through a remotely controlled door and walked with a guard back through empty halls to a cell with six bunk beds, an open toilet, and four or five other men probably decades older than he was. And that was the only "safe" space he had. My mind was spinning.

James's Story

On my second visit that same day, two volunteers and I met a thirty-seven-year-old father of five from Ghana, in West Africa. I will call him James. Like Jorge, James had not broken any US laws. He had legally approached the US border, turned himself in to the border patrol, and requested asylum. We knew from another volunteer who had visited him the previous month that he had been in detention for over a year and a half with no ability to communicate with his wife and children back in West Africa. He had no idea where they were.

When we sat to visit with James at Adelanto that day, his eyes were red and anxious. He was distracted, disconsolate, and desperate. He seemed as ephemeral as a ghost, shifting between our limited conversation (he spoke a dialect of Twi, which we did not, but only very basic English) and then disappearing behind unfocused, distressed eyes—overwhelmed, I imagined, by tumultuous, churning thoughts. He told us his story in bursts, always returning to his present situation, here, in this detention center. He seemed to be continuously searching for a solution: a way out of the detention center, a way into the US, a way to contact his wife, a way to live in safety beyond the reach of his father's death threats, a way to reunite with his children.

We gathered James's story from the pieces of conversation. We learned that to get to the US border with Mexico, James had traveled a common route: from Africa to Brazil, then north across South America, Central America, and Mexico. I think my jaw dropped trying to fathom this journey across three continents and all the countries and borders crossed in between. But for James the journey was simply a matter of fact. He reported just the highlights as if he were reporting a weather forecast.

What motivated him to take that journey to seek asylum in the US? James had fled West Africa to escape his father, a powerful traditionalist priest in Ghana with a large following. James and his wife were Christian. They raised their children in a Christian home. For most of their marriage their Christianity had not been much of a problem. James's father tolerated their religious choice. Problems arose when James's father sought to pass the mantle of his priesthood to his eldest son, James, his heir and successor. James refused. He was a Christian; he could not succeed his father or take charge of the traditionalist congregation. James's father was furious and issued a death threat against him. The full weight and power of his father emboldened members of the congregation to seek James's life, and he had to flee. He left his wife and children behind, believing they were safe. But soon the harassment and threats were too dangerous even for James's family. His wife and children fled their home, and James lost contact with them.

One of our visiting members asked, "Do you have a lawyer?" He said yes. "How is your case progressing?" James told us that it is hard to get the required documents from his home country.

How does one prove a father's persecution from a continent away? Also, James said, he could not sleep. He had pains, and he could not stop his mind from racing. "Do you see a doctor?" Yes, he said. He was taken to the hospital, but there was no translator, or the translator did not speak his dialect of Twi. Even in court, he told us, the translator they found did not use the correct words. He remembered telling a judge how old he was in Twi, and the translator gave the judge the wrong age. So with his little bit of English James corrected the translation for the record.

James told us his asylum case lawyer was doing her best to help. The process was just taking so long. Month after month with no word from his family—how could they find him? And for him to call his hometown in Ghana was not easy. We listened as his talking went in circles—he shifted from talking about not sleeping, to worrying about his wife, to his court case, back to not sleeping, and then to needing medical attention. There was no relief from the constant anxiety about his children. No end to this process of asylum. No way to tell the doctor what he needed. "You are very kind to visit," he told us. "People try. The guards try to help; they teach me English. But no one speaks my language. I have no one."

We changed the subject and asked James what made him happy when he was with his family. Gardening, he said. James loved to garden and grow things. It had been over a year since he had seen a living plant or dug his hands into the earth. He sat for a moment remembering the smell of the ground after the rain and his eyes grew clear, almost peaceful. And then, just as quickly, he came back to the present: just four people sitting in plastic chairs in a visitation room with an armed guard present.

Sending Support from Beyond the Walls

I learned that you cannot send any packages directly to the detention center, but you can send them through Amazon or a book publisher. So I got James's "a" number and the address of the detention center. I ordered a Bible in Twi and English and had it shipped to him. The Bible was all I could think of. That way he could see the Scriptures in his own language and use passages he had memorized to learn and share them in English. Another volunteer who sat with us that day sent him a book on gardening with lush photographs of the trees, flowers, deserts, hills, mountains, and spring poppies that bloom across California. That way, she said, he could at least see a little of the beauty of the America outside of the walls that contained him.

The leader from our Detention Witness group kept in touch with James and visited him a few more times. She encouraged him to hold out through the asylum process, since he had a strong claim that his life was in danger. But James just couldn't do it. His health was not holding up. He had, she reported to me, finally connected with his wife, who was safe in a neighboring African country. Their children were with her. They were fine. But James saw no end to his legal case. He could not secure the documents required, and even if he did, it was unlikely he could bring his family to the US too. And he would not permit them to stay in a detention center like this one to await their immigration hearing. He said he had talked to the guards. They had promised him that if he agreed to be deported, they would not take him back to Ghana. Organizers from Detention Witness were skeptical at this. US policy was to return people to their country of origin if and when they agreed to withdraw their request for asylum and go. But James finally felt he had some control over what was happening to him. He agreed to go.

Choosing Deportation over Detention

Once James signed the papers for "self-deportation," it took DHS (the Department of Homeland Security) another four to six weeks to process the paperwork and to make the arrangements. In that time we were able to collect some clothes, toiletries, and other travel necessities to send with James, who had nothing. We followed the size and weight restrictions on what detainees could carry during deportation—not much, it turns out. One small backpack. I did not get to see James again after that first visit, but I was told that he had received the Bible. I later learned that DHS had indeed taken him straight back to Ghana—policy over promise. But we also learned that he had reunited with his wife and children. They had moved to an undisclosed location in Ghana and hoped they were safe there. So far, so good; they began rebuilding their life, and soon, I hoped, James could plant a garden.

Suffering with Those Who Suffer

Since meeting Jorge and James, I have visited Adelanto multiple times and met many dedicated volunteers. And I will continue to go as I am able. Every time I walk out of the detention center after a visit, the wide-open desert sky feels surreal, almost like an out-of-body experience. A kaleidoscope of emotions builds up during one or two visits and the in-between hours of waiting. After the first trip, my mind was jumping between people, their stories and the details of their stories. I wasn't sure which emotions and images were mine and which ones I had absorbed from being inside those walls, from listening so intensely, from empathizing so deeply. There was claustrophobia. Grief. Anger. Despair. Fear. Frustration. Isolation. Helplessness. More despair. And humility. Humility and also courage. And through it all a kind of desperation that sent people out of their homes to risk everything on the road and then sit behind walls and submit to the mercy of another country's legal system.

No one had prepared me for the humiliation and shame people feel in detention, and yet it was everywhere. To arrive asking for help only to be stripped of one's clothes and personal belongings. To give up every freedom, to be that vulnerable, and then to be treated like a criminal, all the while trying to remember that you are a person, not a criminal. To present yourself at the border and place yourself in someone else's power—this step that immigrants and asylum seekers take is beyond anything I have ever experienced. I struggled to make sense of it.

Christ's Humility: Relinquishing Cosmic Status and Divine Privilege

Then I made the connection. Giving up one's freedom, status, and privilege, accepting vulnerability and humility, putting yourself in someone else's power—this is how the first Christians understood Christ's incarnation.

One of the earliest Christian liturgical traditions is found in Paul's letter to the Philippians (Phil. 2:5–11). Early Christians believed that their God crossed a cosmic border, leaving behind limitless divinity and entering the confines of humanity. The Philippians hymn describes Christ's incarnation as a choice— the actualization of his character, the practice of humility that shapes his life.[12] Christ gives up divinity—the ultimate cosmic status (2:6); he "empties himself" of divine power and freedom (2:7); he accepts humility, vulnerability, and fragility by taking human form (2:7), including the limitations and needs of a physical body, the volatility of human emotions, and the urgency of sensory impressions. Then Christ goes a step further. He puts his life in the hands of others by taking the form of a slave with no right or power to determine his own life; he becomes one who obeys (2:7–8).

Divine humility and vulnerability were unheard-of in first-century deities. Greek, Roman, and Egyptian gods battled and warred against each other to demonstrate their power, control, glory, and status over one another. In Greek and Roman society, to be a free person, answerable to no one but the gods, was the ultimate goal. Freeborn people were ranked highest on the social scale. Their social opposite was the slave. To be a slave in the ancient world was to be utterly dependent on and obedient to one's master, and when the master was not present, to serve any other free person present. To top it all off, Christ's humility and obedience in human form led to his crucifixion, the form of execution Romans reserved only for criminals and slaves.

In this first-century context, Christ's incarnation—giving up divinity, taking the form of a slave, and dying as a criminal—was baffling and utterly absurd. Given the complete reversal of values that Christ embodies and God rewards in the hymn (Phil. 2:9–11), it is amazing that Christian communities preserved it and the theology of the incarnation it presents. But preserve it they did. And, according to Paul, they also strived to embody the same humility, servanthood, and compassionate care that puts others first as a way of practicing "Christ's mind" (2:1–5).

Let the same mind be in you that was in Christ Jesus,

who, though he was in the form of God,
    did not regard equality with God
    as something to be exploited,
but emptied himself,
    taking the form of a slave,
    being born in human likeness.
And being found in human form,
    he humbled himself
    and became obedient to the point of death—
    even death on a cross. (Phil. 2:5–8)

Today, asylum seekers like James and Jorge live out the mind of Christ demonstrated in the divine incarnation. They follow—consciously or not—Christ's trajectory of humility by their willingness to relinquish everything at the border. They may not come from a place of privilege or power, but they are willing to accept a lower status among us, especially in detention, for the opportunity to live here. They submit to US immigration proceedings. They accept the humiliation of being housed like criminals while awaiting the verdict of a legal system under which they have fewer rights than criminals. They endure deprivation and humiliation—stripped of dignity, community, and access to the world. Many don't make it to their hearings. They cannot endure the conditions long enough to see the legal process through to the end, and they self-deport.

Even so, many in the US argue that asylum seekers stay in detention centers because they prefer to take advantage of a free ride in these facilities—paid for by American taxpayers. This is absurd. People get sick in detention; families are separated; mental stability is tested; children die. Asylum seekers are humble people; they do not seek, nor do they deserve, such conditions. They endure the immigration process, hoping that US law will decide in their favor and grant them permission to stay.

Paul quotes the Christ-hymn because he wants the Philippians to imitate Christ's humility and disregard human status and privilege the way Christ does. In his letter Paul praises community members who, like James and Jorge, embody Christ's humility.[13] For example, Epaphroditus risks travel, illness, and death to visit and support imprisoned Christians (Phil. 2:25–27). Welcome Epaphroditus, Paul tells the Philippians, because his solidarity with prisoners embodies Christ (2:29–30). Then there is Timothy, one of Paul's associates in mission. Timothy embodies Christ's humility by serving Paul in prison and by putting the concerns and needs of others before his own (2:20–21). Paul tells the Philippians to welcome people like Timothy because in his service he exemplifies Christ's humility (2:19–22). Paul even tells two of the women leaders in Philippi to agree in Christ by setting aside their differences and finding common ground from which to serve their congregations (4:2–3). In this they are to exercise the mind of Christ.

Paul understands his own circumstances in prison to be a form of embodying the mind of Christ. Paul takes the title "slave" when he writes his letter to the Philippians, insisting that he has no privileges or honor of his own, but that everything he has is Christ's (Phil. 1:1; 3:7–9).[14] In prison, Paul claims that Christ is visible in the chains that Paul wears (1:13) and that Christ is present in physical humiliations and mental degradation: lack of adequate food, clothing, and connection to loved ones (4:10–13). In short, because Christ gave up his divine privileges and took up the most vulnerable human form, Paul follows in Christ's footsteps and, when humiliated, he reinterprets his circumstances as an embodiment of Christ's mind, Christ's humility.

At the center of Paul's letter to the Philippians, he exhorts them to shape their lives according to Christ's mind:

> Do nothing from selfish ambition or conceit, but in humility regard others as better than yourselves. Let each of you look not to your own interests, but to the interests of others. Let the same mind be in you that was in Christ Jesus. (Phil. 2:3–5)

For Paul, having the mind of Christ meant enduring deprivations, shame, and the loss of freedom, status, and privilege in prison. For the Philippian community, embodying the mind of Christ meant relinquishing status and privilege by standing in solidarity with a specific prisoner. The Philippian Christians practiced Christ's humility as a community when they reached out to Paul in prison and sent him financial support, even though they were not wealthy people (4:10–18). Rather than cling to their own political status and safety, they were willing to be associated with Paul, a detained prisoner of the Roman Empire.

Christian communities today embody Christ's humility by relinquishing status and privilege to stand in solidarity with asylum seekers, like Jorge and James, in detention. This effort can feel socially and politically risky. We say we stand with Christ, but are we extending that Christian solidarity to stand with vulnerable detainees, immigrants, and asylum seekers today? Are we practicing Christ's humility by relinquishing our privilege and status on behalf of those suffering in detention centers?

It may not be practical to relinquish our privilege of US citizenship, but we can leverage that citizenship on behalf of others. We can demand a clear immigration process; we can insist on humanitarian responses to those seeking shelter and refugee status at our borders. We can demand that families not be separated, that prisons not be used to house asylum seekers, that children not be detained and further traumatized. We may risk our privilege by advocating for, accompanying, and assisting immigrants. We may be called un-American if we act on behalf of those who do not have legal claims of residence. Yet this is precisely the kind of weakness and vulnerability that Paul claims reveals Christ's power (Phil. 1:12–14; 2 Cor. 12:9–10).

7

Standing before ICE

John 11:1–34

The Pastors' Story

In the spring of 2017 I met a husband and wife pastor team who were seeking community support while they worked to legalize their immigration status. The pastors had arrived in the US over twenty-five years earlier with their two children on a legal visa. They found work and decided to stay. When their visas were nearing expiration, they sought legal counsel to apply for a longer residence. Unfortunately, they engaged an unscrupulous notary public, *un notario*, who promised to file the legal paperwork on their behalf. The Spanish word *notario* refers to a legal functionary, someone who can file legal paperwork before the court as a lawyer would in the US. Of course, in the US, a notary has no authority to represent clients or to file legal paperwork in court. It was a scam. Many Spanish-speaking immigrants who are victimized by *notarios* lose significant sums of money, precious time, and opportunities for legal appeals. That is what happened to these pastors. The notary took their money and disappeared.

When the pastors realized their mistake, they scrambled to raise more money, hire a US lawyer, and meet the deadlines for residence applications. The lawyer they could afford was incompetent. Perhaps he misfiled papers, or missed deadlines, or did not choose the correct procedural path for their situation. They lost more time. But they remained in the US, raising their children, still looking for trustworthy legal help. They worked cleaning houses and offices. They started a church and led mission outreach programs. They served their community, and they worked to save the money to appeal their case.

Eventually the pastors ran out of time and received a deportation order.

They found an excellent local immigration lawyer to appeal the order. When the appeal was denied, and the deportation order was to take effect, they filed for a "stay of deportation"— a legal document[1] granted to undocumented immigrants living in the US who have no criminal record.[2] A stay would extend the amount of time they could remain in the country and is the last-ditch effort in the struggle of many longtime undocumented residents to stay in the US. In their application they demonstrated that they were not a threat to the community but that they contributed to their neighborhood and the stability of their city. They continued their fight to keep their family together and to hold onto their American dream.

A temporary stay of deportation was granted, and the court required the pastors to register with the local ICE office. ICE officials fitted the pastors with ankle bracelets, a bulky GPS system that goes around the ankle, and sent them home. As part of the terms of the stay, the pastors were required to be at their home for a weekly phone call from ICE during a certain window of time. This requirement effectively kept them from any medical appointments or work outside the home for an entire workday. They were also required to come to the ICE office in person for regular check-ins.

For many years they followed the protocol and checked in at the ICE office once every six months. But in the fall of 2017 the time frame changed. ICE officials gave them a shorter, three-month check-in date. At the three-month visit to the ICE office, their stay was renewed for a one-month check-in date, and they were told that further renewal of their stay of deportation was denied. They would need to make preparations to leave the country. After consulting with their lawyer, they decided to make one more appeal.

At this point in their story, our community group learned of the pastors' situation. We are volunteers for a local, Southern California chapter of Clergy and Laity United for Economic Justice (CLUE). The pastors' lawyer, also a member of CLUE, sent out a request to CLUE volunteers to join the pastors and offer moral support on what could be their final ICE check-in. Our goal was simply to let the pastors know that people in their community care what happens to them.

At the check-in, the pastors and their lawyer were going to ask one more time that ICE grant another stay of deportation. The lawyer did not know what would happen. There were several possibilities. The ICE officers could physically take the pastors into custody, separate them, and place them in detention centers to await a decision on their new request. They could be immediately deported. Or the officers could sign the "stay of deportation" paperwork and require them to return in another month to start the process all over again. We did not know if the pastors would go home to have dinner with their children and grandchildren, or if, for the first time in more than thirty years of marriage, they would be separated and then deported without a chance to see their family.

Most Americans do not have to consider the variety of residential statuses, visas, or work permits that these pastors had to navigate. As citizens, we are simply not aware of the numerous, complex legal categories our neighbors and coworkers are living with, renewing, maintaining, and paying for on a regular basis—even when they do have legal permission to be in the country.[3] Once their documents have expired, people enter another vast legal labyrinth to renew residence through a sponsoring relative, through work, or through study in the US. This labyrinth can be stressful, particularly given the time limits, legal costs and requirements, changing government programs for refugees, and establishment and dissolution of resettlement legislation, all with the constant threat of deportation. CLUE and other community organizations can provide information and support to those who live without documentation or are seeking legal status. Such organizations also educate citizens to advocate for the rights of those without legal status. In the case of the pastors, our organization offered personal support.

Accompanying the Pastors: Wednesday Morning, March 7

At 8:30 a.m. on a Wednesday, I joined the twenty or so volunteers from CLUE gathered in a parking lot. We stood outside a small, nondescript office in the middle of a drab business park under cloudy skies. Behind us roared one of the busiest commuter freeways in the nation. In front of us, tucked under a roof that ran along the length of the one-story building, was the local ICE office. The stated mission of this government branch is "to promote homeland security and public safety through the criminal and civil enforcement of federal laws governing border control, customs, trade and immigration."[4] The office was tiny, with barely enough folding chairs along the two office walls to sit more than a handful of immigrants and a couple of lawyers who had accompanied them to their mandated check-in with ICE officials.

In order not to interfere with ICE business, our cheerful group remained outside the small office, leaving a clear path to the entrance. Inside we could see a bank teller's window in one of the walls. It had thick glass with an opening at the bottom to slide relevant documents through and one of those raspy speakers so the officer on the inside could hear the person on the outside, and vice versa. It was surreal—the regular, dull roar of traffic on the highway contrasting with the quiet footfalls of people approaching this office to hear decisions that could change their lives.

The ICE office opened at nine o'clock. We arrived early so we could welcome and encourage the pastors when they arrived to make their appeal. They had been coming regularly to this office, or one like it, for over a decade, complying with the legal requirements, accompanied by their lawyer. They knew almost all of the officers by name and disposition. The lawyer mentioned that she had been here maybe three or four times a month with her clients.

The clergy gathered on one side of the ICE office entrance—a Reform rabbi, an Episcopal priest, a Lutheran pastor, a Unitarian minister, a nondenominational evangelical pastor, and a Presbyterian pastor. On the other side of the entrance stood many more brothers and sisters of many faith commitments and traditions, ethnicities, and backgrounds. Three members of the pastors' own congregation were also present. Under gray clouds, the color and warmth of the day came from the people gathered and the signs we held: a rainbow of hearts and the simple word "love" in cursive script printed from a home computer.

The faith volunteers greeted folks we recognized from the trainings we had attended over the past two weeks. We introduced ourselves, connected with our organizational leaders, and passed around the heart/love signs. To be clear, we were not protesting. We were not threatening. We wore smiles and tried to project friendly energy. We were there simply to stand with and support two pastors as they filed for another stay of deportation.

When a few ICE officers arrived for work, they may have recognized the short, curly-haired young lawyer standing with us. Or perhaps the officers were feeling friendly or just wanted to test for any tension in our crowd. They smiled as they made their way across the parking lot to work, some even called out hello. We waved and called back morning greetings, commenting on the gray skies and possible rain. Like the officers, we conveyed our presence without antagonism. I appreciated that gesture from both groups—the exchange of pleasantries as we all got down to our work. We CLUE volunteers were organized and low-key. We had no media with us, no cameras or cell phones directed at the office. We were there *for* the couple, not *against* anyone. Still, the ICE officials could have responded in any number of ways, including ignoring us. They chose to acknowledge us with a gracious hello, and we responded in kind.

That mutual respect and recognition felt right. These men and women were doing their jobs. As citizens and neighbors from the community, we were doing ours. Our interfaith group prayed together outside. We laid hands on the undocumented pastors before they went into the office to present their written appeal, and then we stood outside on the sidewalk in the parking lot and sang while we waited for the news. People came and went. People approached the window in the office, passed papers through the little slot, sat down again or left. We waited. We sang. We prayed. We bore witness.

Finally, after all of the other people checking in had left the office, the lawyer and the pastors stood up, opened the door, and came out onto the sidewalk. They seemed stunned, almost expressionless. We couldn't tell whether the news was good or bad. Later I understood that they were attempting to process what they had heard. They did not know how to react—was this a win or a loss? The lawyer attempted to speak, grasping for the right words and trying to say something concrete, something definitive. But the ICE officer had made no decision.

He had referred the case to the Los Angeles office, kicking the can down the road for two more weeks. This meant the pastors had two more weeks here with their family—that was a win. But without a decision to approve the stay of deportation, the deportation order was now in effect, and they were required to make arrangements to leave the country. The officer told them to purchase their airplane tickets and "wrap up their affairs." They would wait two more weeks to see whether the LA office would grant the stay; meanwhile, they were in limbo, waiting at the border between losing everything and gaining permission to stay a little longer. Two more weeks to fan a spark of hope one hardly dared to express.

We surrounded the pastors outside the ICE office and physically held them. I remember that the *pastora* stumbled back under some unseen weight. She sagged against me. The Episcopal priest standing on her other side pressed in, and between us, we held her up and kept her from collapsing on the pavement. The pastor asked the rabbi to pray, as she had prayed for them before. She lifted the prayer *tallit* and wrapped it around them, husband and wife, forming a tent over them. It was as if her gesture and her prayer became the arms of God enveloping and sheltering these weary immigrants just as God had sheltered Naomi and Ruth in their time of uncertainty. Her prayer in Hebrew lifted over the pastors and drew all of us into that shelter where God's wings (Ruth 2:12) know no limits or weakness, where the borders to blessings and restrictions to grace dissolve before the one Creator who gives refuge to all.

Stretching across Borders and Boundaries to Offer Shelter

The geopolitical, social-ethnic, and religious borders we sometimes cling to are not divine. They are human creations, based on organizational principles that are fallible and, too often, tainted with stereotypes or shaped by partisan economic interests, or are products of devastating racial and gender assumptions. When, for example, geopolitical borders are managed for the safety of all humans, they should be respected. But when such borders divide families, devastate community resources, and destroy people's lives and health, Jesus's teaching mandates that we step across those borders to stand with people in need. That morning, standing in the ICE office parking lot, we disagreed with the ways the immigration laws were being applied, but we respected the legal borders and the roles of law officials. We complied with the law. *And* we reached across denominational, religious, and perhaps a host of other borders to hold two people in prayer as they complied, heartbreakingly, with the legal processes.

I also know that in another time and place, these Christian pastors and I might have met over a church coffee hour and entered into a theological discussion. I sensed that my understanding of salvation and theirs are quite different. As a Christian standing among brothers and sisters of many faiths and humanist traditions, I knew we might have deeply disagreed on particular religious or doctrinal borders. We might have respectfully come to disagree about specific beliefs, church confessions, and definitions of sin, morality, and ethics—even the possibility of salvation. But given the opportunity to stand in solidarity both physically and spiritually with our brother and sister in their time of need, there was no hesitation. We crossed those borders of faith and belief that so often divide people.

Navigating Legal Limbo

That afternoon, I received an email update from the CLUE office. The organizers thanked people for their time accompanying the pastors and assured us that our presence had made a difference, even though the ultimate outcome was unclear. "The pastors themselves were considerably heartened at the sight and sound and sometimes actual physical support from our group. The power of prayer is real!"[5]

The email was sent out to confirm what those of us who had been there Wednesday morning already knew—there was no final resolution. We learned that the pastors must return in person in two weeks with their one-way airplane tickets to a country they had not visited in decades and that they no longer called home. This would demonstrate that they were complying with the deportation order and were ready to leave the country if the stay was not granted. The pastors continued to comply with weekly phone check-ins from ICE officials. They continued to wear the cumbersome ankle bracelet. And now the pastors began to wrap up their affairs. They quit their cleaning jobs, giving the work to others who could take their places. They consolidated their belongings and moved in with their son. During the day they watched their grandchildren while their son and daughter-in-law now worked to provide for two additional adults on considerably less family income.

Preparing to Accompany the Pastors a Second Time

Prior to the pastors' return visit to the ICE office, volunteers attended another training session. We were told what to expect and how to conduct ourselves. The lawyer also reminded us that the pastors' case was not public. No pictures, no media presence, no use of names or identifying details in social media. Understandably, the pastors had requested privacy to protect their family members and the members of their largely immigrant congregation. Still, their resistance to "going public" was difficult for some of our activist volunteers to understand. We knew that public pressure was one of the strongest tools we could wield on behalf of the pastors. Some CLUE members voiced concern that our supporting presence was not enough— that we needed to do more. The lawyer tried to explain the pastors' adamant position. They did not want publicity, she said, because any public knowledge of their personal situation felt shameful and humiliating. Treated as criminals by the law, they did not want their friends, relatives, employers, or church members to see them as criminals. This was important for us to hear. While we volunteers thought of the pastors' situation as a question of justice, pointing to an immigration system in need of reform, we had to remember that the people caught in this system feel isolated, humiliated, and dehumanized by the experience. Standing with them on their terms is one way we could support their human dignity.

The Pastors' Dilemma

When I first met the pastor in his church, I asked him if he had told his congregation what he was going through. He said this was a real dilemma for him and for his wife. "We haven't told them," he replied. "Only a few people know, and they are supporting us. But many others would not understand. They hear about ICE and they are afraid. They might think I am a criminal or drug dealer because I am involved with the ICE officers, or because they see I am wearing an ankle bracelet. It doesn't matter that I am trying to follow the laws and get my documents in order."

In another conversation, the pastor admitted he was conflicted by his own role as pastor: "It is so difficult," he told me. "The members of the church who know about our status and our deportation struggle are trying to comfort me, but that is my job—to *comfort them* as their pastor. How can I care for my flock if I am asking them to take care of me?" In his words I heard resonances of a deeper, unspoken concern the pastor carried with him: "If I am deported, who will pastor them? How can I abandon my congregation?" Knowing what his members had suffered, the pastor could not bear to add his suffering to their plates, and to think of leaving them without a church or spiritual guide was agonizing for him.

Accompanying Immigrants through Legal Limbo

Standing on the legal border between being in or out of the US is an excruciating limbo. For two weeks, the pastors could do nothing but get their affairs in order, walking forward one day at a time, filing paperwork and meeting deadlines while serving their congregation, working odd jobs for income, and babysitting their grandchildren. For the lawyer, the pastors' case was one among many. Every case involved people with hopes, fears, lives, loved ones, and unique stories. The lawyer walked with her clients through their legal journey until every effort was exhausted or security in the US was won, and then she moved on to the next case, win or lose.

The citizen volunteers from CLUE who accompanied the pastors saw only the smallest glimpse of an immigrant's experience. We gave a couple of hours from our week and then went back to work, following our routines and schedules, stepping in and out of awareness of the pastors' legal limbo. Living in this limbo is not sustainable. We knew the pastors would end up on one side of the border or the other, either deportees or US residents for another time period. The lawyer would continue representing clients, winning some cases and losing others. And the volunteers? What would we do? How could our congregations help?

Reflecting on that morning, I could see two opportunities for faith communities. The first is to actively accompany our neighbors by exercising the "golden rule" to "Love your neighbor as yourself" (Lev. 19:18; Matt. 22:39).[6] We can love our neighbors by walking with them as they navigate the immigration process and the legal limbo. This is love in the act of accompaniment. When we walk with others, we hear their stories and we share our stories. We learn how other people experience America.

Love as active accompaniment requires physically showing up and being there. It is a public, bodily witness. For Christians, loving our neighbors through a ministry of accompaniment is one way to imitate Christ. Christ took human form in order to walk with us through the experience of being human—through the physical suffering and the joy.[7]

The second opportunity is for faith communities to enter into the spiritual practice of being present to those who are psychically suffering. Active accompaniment—loving our neighbors in concrete ways over the long haul—can be exhausting, frustrating, and full of ambiguity. Often, concrete, public actions are not possible. As human beings and as Christians, we need to also practice being emotionally present with others in the ambiguity of their situations without jumping to solutions or actions or platitudes. We can learn the spiritual practice of simply being present with our neighbors, particularly when it is uncomfortable. Standing in places of existential discomfort, we come to appreciate the "thin places," places of deep connection, insight, and self-knowledge, that offer proximity to one another and the divine. Standing with one another in the difficult and ambiguous thin places during those times and circumstances when we cannot take action, we learn to wait and be still, hearing, feeling, and seeing all that is in the present moment. And although we may not be able to change the injustice, we can bear witness and testify by our physical presence and spiritual solidarity.

Wednesday Morning, March 21

The weather forecast for the pastors' last ICE visit was rain. We were prepared. We returned in large numbers, dressed in boots, hats, umbrellas, and other gear. People sported now-soggy heart signs, and we sang hymns in English and Spanish, read Scripture, and shared inspirational readings to encourage the pastors who were seated inside the ICE office, just a few feet away on the other side of the picture windows. At one point the lawyer stepped out to tell us they could hear us singing and felt encouraged, so we continued to lift our voices.

After over an hour, the lawyer came out and gave us the update: it would be another hour or so of waiting. The Los Angeles ICE office had reviewed the case and denied the pastors a stay of deportation. The LA office directive stipulated that the pastors would have to leave the US on April 6, the date of their scheduled one-way flight on the tickets they had purchased the previous week to comply with the deportation order. But after some conversation and insistence, the local ICE officers in this small regional office told the lawyer they would review the case handed back from the LA office one more time. This would take about an hour.

An excruciating hour. A hopeful hour. A deceptive hour. Standing together and waiting is inherent to Christian testimony, the spiritual witness in most faith traditions, and also in community action for justice. I thought of the women gathered on a hilltop overlooking the crucifixion grounds on Good Friday (Mark 15:40–41). They couldn't stop the death that was coming. They couldn't hold off their imminent loss or the suffering. They couldn't intervene in the inevitable end of Jesus's *via crucis*. But they were there. They didn't flee. They stood vigil. They accompanied Jesus the only way they could. They witnessed by their presence and offered silent testimony. We did the same.

The decision didn't take an hour. The paperwork was passed through the little slot in the window after a mere twenty minutes. The pastors and the lawyer took the papers, stood, turned, and came outside to meet us. The lawyer spoke. There was no change to the LA office decision, no reprieve, no stay of deportation. The pastors must leave the country in two weeks, on April 6; they must continue reporting weekly to ICE. We should let them go home now. So, after quick, stunned hugs, the pastors walked to their truck. The husband held the door for his wife and helped her in. They fastened their seat belts and drove home.

We regrouped on one side of the building, away from the parking lot. The lawyer prepared to speak. But what more was there to say? She had done all she could within the bounds of law, yet the order for deportation remained in place. There were no more legal options for appeal. It made no difference to remind the officers one more time that within twelve to eighteen months the pastors' son, who had a green card and had married a US citizen, could apply and receive citizenship. At that point, if the pastors had remained in the country, their son could have legally sponsored their application for citizenship. Once they were deported, regardless of their son's status, they were prohibited from entering the US again for ten years. What was one more year of deferred deportation after a twenty-four-year fight to keep a family together?

Even as she reviewed for us the final legal steps she and the pastors had taken, the lawyer was still thinking. Since they could not appeal for another stay, perhaps the local congresswoman could contest the removal order on the pastors' behalf. The congresswoman had expressed support for their case. Alternatively, the pastors could seek sanctuary in a house of worship. That move depended on the willingness of ICE to respect public houses of worship and the willingness of the pastors to take such a public step. CLUE members and local faith communities had some experience with sanctuary. In 2007, Liliana Santuario, as she was known in the media, was a young mother who sought sanctuary and lived in a United Church of Christ congregation for three years.[8] Entering and maintaining sanctuary is not easy. Liliana's husband and children were only able to live with her in the church for some of that time. Volunteers from the congregation and community committed to accompanying Liliana twenty-four hours a day. Protestors marched, carried signs, and kept noisy vigil outside the church, shouting "Go home, Liliana!" and worse. Still, local sanctuary efforts have kept people safe, contained, visible to the public, and, when possible, in relatively close proximity to family, friends, and supporters. There is nothing barring federal agents from entering any house of prayer or place of worship and removing someone from the premises. Historically, however, "US Immigration and Customs Enforcement has a long-standing policy of generally avoiding enforcement activities at 'sensitive locations' such as churches, hospitals and schools."[9] This policy has yet to be tested under the Trump administration. The person in sanctuary remains in the US and can have visits from family and friends while their legal case moves through the courts. Sanctuary is a community's prophetic act of accompaniment in public view. The act demands sacrifices from all participants and offers no guarantee of the desired outcome: keeping families together legally in the US.

The pastors had been reluctant to enter sanctuary, even if a willing congregation could be quickly identified, trained, and prepared. The pastors would be completely dependent on their supporters and advocates for food, shelter, and resources. They would not be able to work or continue their ministry. The sanctuary space might be in a city or town at a fair distance from their family. But perhaps with this final denial from ICE and imminent removal, they would consider sanctuary. The lawyer would contact our organizers and let us know if there was a final Hail Mary[10] we could throw to keep the pastors in the US with their family. We would continue that conversation by email, out of the rain.

Monday, March 26

The Hail Mary

Five days later, on the afternoon of March 26, I read in an email that the pastors' lawyer was working with the congresswoman to make yet another request for a stay on the basis of community leader support. The lawyer asked for volunteers—particularly clergy—to write letters on institutional letterhead, to use our titles and sign in ink rather than electronically, and to deliver the letters to her office by 5:00 p.m. I had one hour. I drafted a letter in support of the pastors. I printed and signed the letter. I got in my car and drove to the lawyer's office. I walked into the office at a quarter to five and came face-to-face with the pastors, seated on a sofa in a small, comfortable waiting room.

The last time I had seen them, they were driving away from the ICE office in the rain. Now, five days later, they were here for one more try—a last-ditch effort. They had finalized preparations to leave the country, even as they harbored some glimmer of hope they might be able to stay. They were still living with their son and his family, but they were no longer able to contribute to the rent. This was deeply troubling for the pastors. Their difficulties were making circumstances even more tenuous for their son. Rental costs are high in Southern California. For families living at the economic margins, it takes multiple incomes to make ends meet, especially for those with small children.

Medical bills had increased their economic burden. The pastors had come to the lawyer's office directly from the doctor's office. The *pastora*'s health was deteriorating. I wasn't surprised; they had been under increasing and overwhelming daily stress since August. I didn't ask for details, but it sounded like a heart condition aggravated by successive waves of stress, worsening incrementally as their legal process grew bleaker. Had the pastor told his congregation about their legal status, his wife's precarious health, or the impending deportation? "No, they still don't know," he replied. He was a proud, self-made man who had always provided for his family and trusted God's grace. As the head of household he felt ashamed, as if he were letting his family down, needing their care instead of providing for them. He did not want to feel that shame as a pastor standing before his congregation, even if it meant leaving his flock in the dark and without a proper goodbye.

God's Word in Scripture

A few moments passed, and the pastor brightened a bit. Even with all of these trials, he said, he remembered that Saint Paul had also suffered at the hands of authorities and found power in that suffering. The pastor told me that he, like Paul, had been newly emboldened in his preaching. He sat forward on the sofa with a new light in his eyes to tell me the message he had preached the previous week. Beside him, the *pastora* leaned back, closed her eyes, and grew still as she listened, every now and then chiming in with an "Amen" and "Praise God."

"Sunday's Scripture was the story of Lazarus," he began. "You know it, I'm sure. Lazarus dies and he is lying in the grave, his feet and hands bound with cloth. And Jesus comes, traveling to see him with his disciples. The disciples think Lazarus is sleeping, but Jesus knows what has happened, and Jesus has a purpose." "Praise God!" added the *pastora* from the couch.

The pastor continued: "And as he gets closer to the tomb, Jesus sees the people, and he sees the boulder rolled across the entrance. And I thought, that is what has happened to us! We were alive, moving, walking, talking, working, and raising our family, but now a giant boulder has been rolled across our lives, keeping us from moving forward, restricting our ministry and our abilities to make a living. The boulder is too big; we can't move it by ourselves. So we called on the community, and you came, and the rabbi came, and many, many others like the lawyer and the pastors all came to help move the boulder—but we cannot do it alone. Only Christ can move that boulder!"

As the pastor spoke, the *pastora* and I felt the energy of his message and the power of the Scriptures, as if the Spirit caught hold of Lazarus's story and animated it before our eyes. I could see all of us—the activists, the lawyer, the supporters—standing at Lazarus's tomb, pushing on that boulder to make a way for God to raise the dead from the grave. In that vision, the rock heaved aside, leaving a gaping hole as the smell of the dead released into the air. The pastor summoned more energy and described Jesus approaching the tomb. The pastor's face shone, and he pronounced the words of the Lord: "*Lazaro, levántate!*" ("Lazarus, come out!"). Two simple words in Spanish. "This is the command of God to raise the dead," cried the pastor, leaning into his vision as he shared the message.

"Then," he said, "I realized that these papers, this appeal here in my hand, they are Lazarus. Last week they were dead in the tomb, sealed away with no life in them. And we were grieving, we had no hope; we could see no future. But then we called on Jesus, and he has said to these papers, 'Get up! Rise up and come into the light! Leave behind the wraps and cloths and step into the sun. Bring life and breath again to this family.' We were dead, but Jesus is with us. The Lord will never fail us, he has a purpose for us and for our ministry. We will never stop praising his way and his purpose. We will never let go of our faith. This"—he shakes the papers at me—"this is our Lazarus!"

"Amen!" we say together. "Amen!" echoes the *pastora* on the couch.

I left my letter of support with the pastors. The lawyer would add it to the documents, letters of support, and testimonies to push against that rock. The next day, a volunteer would convey the paperwork and letters to the LA ICE office. That was the Hail Mary, our hope for resurrecting the pastors' American life.

My Letter of Support

March 26, 2018

Dear Field Office Director,

My name is Julia Lambert Fogg, and I am writing in support of the two pastors who are filing a final appeal for a stay to their deportation order. I am writing in conjunction with my congresswoman's office, the lawyer's legal office, and the support of many local pastors, rabbis, neighbors, and community members.

I am a professor at California Lutheran University, where I have taught in the religion department since 2003. I have served as chair of the faculty, and I have served on the Board of Regents at Cal Lutheran. I have also chaired the Cal Lutheran religion department for seven years.

I am a pastor. I have faithfully served my presbytery and regional churches since 2004. I have also served a number of Lutheran congregations in Southern California over the past decade.

The pastors are two of the most committed, gentle, and faithful Christian people I know. For their entire twenty-four years in the U.S., from legally entering the country, through the deception and theft committed by those posing as legal representatives that led to multiple missed opportunities to legalize their permanent residency, to their continued ministry to people living at the margins in California, the pastors have maintained clear, open, and regular communications with ICE. They have conformed to every legal requirement for their movement and schedule. They are an incredible witness to Christ, to Christian character and morality, and to family values.

I have been working with people like the pastors for many years, and I am crushed by the news that this husband and wife will not be able to stay in their community to continue the ministry that they have faithfully built over the last twenty years. I have met members of their congregation, and I have seen their work, their faith, and their commitment to helping people manage daily difficulties, all within the bounds of the law. I appeal to you to grant these pastors a legal stay of deportation so that they may continue their work to strengthen our community and to walk with the members of their congregation.

Thank you for your time, for all the work you do to keep our country safe, and for your own personal sacrifice to uphold our American values of a strong country made up of loyal families.

The Rev. Dr. Julia Lambert Fogg
Professor of Religion

Tuesday, March 27

The news came in emails as we waited to hear what would happen.

Friends,

As you already know, with the support of our congressmember, the pastors will be filing one more stay request. A dear friend sought to file this stay request early this morning on their behalf, but was rebuffed. The LA ICE office insisted that the pastors themselves appear to make the filing. Although this has not been a requirement in the past (in fact, when last month's stay request was accepted for filing, the pastors were NOT present), the ICE Officer on duty this morning demanded their physical presence.

In an abundance of caution, we are calling upon all people of good faith to accompany the pastors tomorrow morning as they file their stay request, to ensure that they are supported and that we can be witnesses to any adverse actions that might be taken against them.

—The pastors' attorney[11]

Wednesday, March 28

Friends,

Today two volunteers accompanied the pastors and me, along with another attorney, as we fought to have Immigration and Customs Enforcement (ICE) in Los Angeles accept our request for a stay of removal. Many, many thanks to a local rabbi for so promptly providing the filing fees for the applications. Honestly, as we headed into Los Angeles this morning, we were seriously concerned that the pastors might be detained and summarily removed from the country.

Nevertheless, it was important that we have the stay filed, so that our congressmember's office might advocate on our behalf with ICE to approve a pending petition. Her office is working to do this now.

Of the many, many miracles which occurred today, the brightest one was that, upon leaving the federal building, together, we came upon the scene of "Mateo25"[12] and their public fast in support of another pastor through his ICE check-in.

The miraculous thing about our being there at the same time as the Mateo25 group was that among the coordinators of this action in Los Angeles was another pastor-activist, one of the key strategists behind Liliana Santuario's campaign to remain here in the United States with her family. To feel the spirit of our own pastors lift as they saw the diversity and joy of the folks gathered in support of another pastor was a thing of wonder. The pastors felt all the love, care, and prayers of our circle, keeping each of you in their thoughts as we waited throughout the morning to see what might happen. And now to know that we are part of a larger movement, we are another thread in the tapestry of people around the nation seeking justice, demanding humane treatment for all our brothers and sisters—this was an unexpected gift today.

The pastors are very hopeful that our congressmember's office can help. We are focused on their securing a stay of removal for another year. We do not have a sense of when we might have an answer. It might be tonight, it might come on the eve of the pastors' scheduled departure, on April 6th. We continue to hope and pray, together, across all faith traditions (and even NO faith traditions) and throughout Southern California. Please continue to keep their story in your heart, and share with friends and family during this holiday season what this witness has meant to you.

We ask that all those involved continue to keep the names, church, and country of origin of the pastors confidential. We are not yet ready to speak with the media.

Thank you to so many of you who wrote beautiful letters in support of the pastors. And on behalf of myself and the pastors, we wish you a happy Easter and happy Pesach.

—The pastors' attorney

Wednesday, April 6

Dear Friends,

This has been an extremely difficult journey, with truly amazing moments of joy and hope and also terrible moments of despair. The whole experience has been rich and more full of love through the care of each and every one of you, the local members of CLUE.

We got terrible news early last Friday morning. The last-minute stay was denied. Many CLUE members wrote letters of support and accompanied us to the ICE office. Indivisible[13] groups also joined, as did CLUE-LA. Nevertheless, last Friday, we received a message directly from the on-duty ICE director denying the stay. He tried to frame the decision as "business as usual," reasonable since the pastors had already been granted previous stays and therefore could not expect any further delay. What wasn't said was how enforcement has changed in the last year, from prioritizing deportations of serious threats to our communities to "deport them all."

The stay denial was a terrible blow because the pastors were less than two years away from being able to legalize their status here. They have been wonderful, contributing members of our society, having lived here most of their adult lives and having raised their children here. They had been waiting on results of medical tests to finalize a medical diagnosis. Once outside the United States, they will not be allowed to return for any reason for ten years—even once their son becomes a US citizen and files for them. The ICE director was aware of the stakes involved, but new administration enforcement priorities leave little room for discretion—everyone is being pushed out.

Given this decision, there was no good or easy answer. Ultimately, the pastors complied with the ICE rules and left for their "home" country in South America on Friday night. At the end, a volunteer pastor stayed in contact with them for us and leads the effort to find them some money to help them start over after nearly a quarter century living here. They have no close relatives in their country. These next few weeks will likely be very difficult for them and for their children and grandchildren here in the US.

Thanks to so many pledging support, we were able to send them off with some initial funds, but doubtless their need will continue until they make a new life in South America.

They, and I, thank you profoundly for all your care, efforts, prayers, and support. I cannot help but think of the exodus story at this

Passover season, and the lessons that story seeks to teach us about exile and the folly of persecuting "the stranger."

The journey continues. Others need our help, including our commitment to stopping the deportation machine and to enacting a new, humane immigration law that honors the struggles of those who must leave the lands of their birth and who, once here, contribute so much to the rich fabric of US society.

Please stay with us.

—The pastors' attorney

Death and Resurrection: John 11:1–44

I read the line again and again: "Ultimately, the Pastors complied with the ICE rules and left on Friday night." One line to note the end of two lives lived in America. I remembered the pastor's sermon on Lazarus, the man Jesus raised from the dead. Lazarus too was the breadwinner of the family, leaving behind his sisters, Mary and Martha, a household, and perhaps even the family business when he passed. But Jesus raised him from the dead. I finally understood the devastation and accusation in Martha's voice when she said to Jesus, "Lord, if you had been here, my brother would not have died" (John 11:21). Where was Jesus when the sisters needed him to hold their family, their livelihood, their community standing, and their well-being together? Where was Jesus when the pastors and their family needed him now?

I took out my Bible and read the Lazarus passage in John's Gospel again. The pastor and his wife were devastated, I knew. I also knew that they would cling to their faith and look for Jesus to guide them as they tried to find their feet on South American ground, starting over with nothing. Jesus had told Martha, "I am the resurrection and the life. Those who believe in me, even though they die, will live" (11:25). Perhaps the pastors heard Jesus's reply to Martha—"Your brother will rise again"—as a promise to them as well (11:23). Their life in America was dead, and their family would live on here in the States without them. I prayed that there was still life ahead for them, that they might know Lazarus's resurrection.

Reflections on the Promise of Resurrection

As a Christian, I believe in the resurrection of the dead. I confess a God who has created all that is, who has given breath and life to all living beings, and who sustains that life—all life—with justice and compassion. As a Christian, I confess that human beings know much less than we think we do. We make mistakes, we break laws—human and divine. We are caught in systems of sin, and by our actions we destroy the life and lives with which God has blessed us. Our neighbors, whether we know them or not, are gifts of God, precious in God's eyes, worthy of our respect, love, compassion, protection, and goodwill.

For some concerned Americans, the pastors we stood with had broken US law—not by entering the country, since they had entered legally, but by overstaying the legal terms of their residence and by failing to correct their legal status in a timely manner. For them, the fact that the pastors had been seeking to legalize their residency but were taken advantage of by predatory people does not resolve their illegal status. Indeed, the pastors knew, just as I know, that being victims of a crime is not an excuse. Still, it was a fact of their case and was one reason US officials had permitted them to remain in the country for so long.

As a Christian, I hope and believe that the pastors are experiencing God's resurrection power in their country of birth. Twice they were made refugees—once as new parents leaving their first home, and now as grandparents leaving their US home. Yet, with God's help, they may still emerge from their quarter-century-long tomb of deadly anxiety, fear, doubt, and struggle. Months or years from now, when they are reestablished—if they ever are—they may stumble out of the tomb and into the light. April 2028, a decade after their removal, is the first possible date they can reapply for a visa to visit their family in the US.

But right now I imagine the pastors, like Jesus or Mary and Martha, walking the way of the cross, *la via dolorosa*, abandoned by the promise of life in the US. Their American life was wrapped in a funeral cloth and placed in a tomb. They left their family and returned to an unknown country where they had no home, no resources, and no social network or kin. The US law was executed, demonstrating that there is no longer room for compassion in deportation decisions. But the law is human, and human laws can be changed. As a citizen of the United States, I respect our laws; I also want to stand with those who work to find a way to safely raise their families. I believe our legal system can and should distinguish between criminal offenders and people who do everything within their means to follow our laws. I want no part in this separation of families, this emotional death, this spiritual loss, this overwhelming grief.

Jesus was ultimately willing to walk the way of the cross. He also walked that way with Lazarus's sisters rather than leave them to walk through their loss alone. Jesus knew that Lazarus was dead when he decided to go to Mary and Martha in Bethany. There was nothing he could do to heal Lazarus. Jesus's disciples advised against going. They knew of the danger Jesus was in. Officials from Jerusalem were looking to kill him, and Bethany was deep in their territory. "Rabbi, the Jews were just now trying to stone you, and are you going there again?" (John 11:8). When Jesus insisted, Thomas encouraged the other disciples, "Let us also go, that we may die with him" (11:16).

Jesus risked his life to be with Mary and Martha in their loss, and his disciples went to die with him.

This story is incredible to me for the compassion Jesus showed his friends, the two sisters. He was with them in their grief. He wept with them (11:35). He allowed himself to be moved by their loss. And even though he had other plans, he honored their grief and shared their pain (11:20–37). Jesus taught his disciples about taking political risk in order to accompany others—that it's worth it. Even when death or deportation is inevitable, walking with a family through the brokenness they are experiencing is worth it.

The pastors we were walking with reminded me of what Jesus taught his disciples about resurrection hope. Resurrection hope is not logical or guaranteed. It is miraculous but does not always come when we need or expect it. Resurrection hope does not follow rules. It does not obey prayer vigils or political agendas. Resurrection hope is a prophetic hope. It names injustice in order to call it out. This is the first step on the way to justice. Resurrection hope intensifies the prophetic witness against unjust laws, even when we lose in court. Resurrection hope manifests like the mustard seed—a weed that grows out of control. It prickles and itches. It offends and will not be eradicated. And then when it carpets the hillsides with brilliant colors and textures after the spring rains, it illuminates a new world. I want to be a part of that resurrection hope.

8

Where Do We Go from Here?
Border Crossing as Praxis

John 1:1–5, 14

This chapter outlines a few ways for faith groups, communities, and individuals to open our hearts, minds, and resources to our immigrant neighbors living within the US borders. I'd like to begin with a very basic exercise for citizens who have not experienced forced immigration. This is a first step in developing and cultivating our understanding and empathy for others by beginning with ourselves. The first step toward empathy for people who are crossing borders is for us to get comfortable with crossing borders. And to do that, we need to practice getting out of our comfort zone.[1]

Step 1: Getting Out of Our Comfort Zones

Practice Being a Guest

Consider, for example, the difference in your comfort level when you host people in your home, church, or community group and when you are a guest in someone else's home, religious center (their church, mosque, synagogue, gurdwara, temple, or spiritual gathering place), or community group. It is a lot of work to invite people into your house—the cooking, cleaning, and preparing, making sure you have enough chairs, cutlery, activities for children, conversation topics, signage for people arriving, and so forth. There is a lot to do. But all that preparation is in your control, left up to your choices and preferences. It may be busy and overwhelming, but you choose the food, the space, the people, and the arrangements. In these ways, hosting someone in your own place and space and at your own rhythm is easy.

When you are a guest, however, the arrangements are not in your hands. Being a guest requires that we put ourselves (our dietary needs, allergies, thirst, sociability, rhythms, and expectations) in someone else's hands. We arrive on their turf. We must adjust to their cooking style and the smells coming from the kitchen,[2] their effusive or more reticent welcome, their level of formality or informality, their rhythm of conversation and play, their family dynamics, their sense of roles and expectations, their forms of address, their cultural assumptions, and the rules of the house. For example, shoes may be on or off inside, and different protocols determine who eats first, who tells the stories, and how gender and age distinctions are made at the table. Learning to be a good guest, particularly in the home or community space of people from another cultural background, I suggest, is essential to learning how to behave and relax with people when we are outside of our own comfort zone. Learning to be a good guest by sharing other people's foods, ideas, cultures, protocols, and families is one way to practice border crossing.

How often are you a guest in someone else's house? How often are you and your family guests in another house of faith? How often do you attend community cultural events that your neighbors are hosting and that are open to the public? These public events might be a festival for a saint's day of the congregation up the street; a harvest celebration (strawberries, corn, spring, foundation day, new moon, etc.); or a play or choir performance by a congregation, faith community, or cultural organization that is different from your usual social or cultural comfort zone with friends and neighbors. Attending these public events is another way to practice being a guest and getting outside the borders of your comfort zone. It is an accessible way to begin stretching your cultural borders and learning other peoples' traditions of eating, gathering together, and celebrating.

Step Out of Our Liturgical Spaces

Next you might consider getting out of your liturgical comfort zone and sharing prayer or worship with another church or faith community that offers to receive you. You could attend an open mosque day or a Baha'i event to serve the community. These events don't have to be worship settings—in fact, it's better if they are not. But many culturally centered churches, mosques, synagogues, gurdwaras, Hindu temples, and other faith organizations often advertise cultural celebrations in religious spaces that are open to the public.[3] They *want* you to come. They are eager to share their traditions on days when they host these gatherings. Instead of playing it safe and returning to familiar events, seek out local cultural celebrations and get to know your neighbors on their cultural turf, in their own contexts and comfort zones. You have nothing to lose except a social or cultural border that you probably were not even aware was restricting you.

As you read this, do you feel a little anxious or resistant to these ideas? Are you experiencing a little discomfort? Have you thought, "I wouldn't be welcome" or "I might say the wrong thing and offend my hosts" or "My home congregation wouldn't understand"? Good. That *discomfort* means you are stepping out of the boundaries of your comfort zone. And yes, you might indeed say something wrong or ask an awkward, though innocent, question. Good. That means you are imagining how to stretch the borders of your comfort zone, and you are exploring how it would feel to be genuinely interested in people who are different from you *on their own turf*. You are taking a step toward a willingness to be vulnerable and make mistakes and learn from others when they are willing to teach you their ways. When people prepare to receive guests—either in their own homes, in their houses of prayer, or in their cultural community centers—they are ready to invite you in. They want to engage well-meaning, open, curious outsiders who come with questions about their place or space.

Experiencing our own trepidation at not doing things quite right in someone else's home or on someone else's cultural turf is good practice for all of us. In these spaces we learn that people can be very generous to us when we are willing to be their guests. Start here. Learn to be a guest in someone else's house and stretch your borders. Lean out of your cultural comfort zone and try something that expands your circle of neighbors. Don't expect other people to fit into your expectations or to do things the way you do them. The whole point of this practice is to get comfortable with someone else's way of doing things.[4]

Step 2: Listening Broadly to Other Voices and Experiences

Ready for a second step? Once you have stretched your comfort zone and widened its borders, invite more voices and perspectives into your view of your hometown or your understanding of the world. Because of social media, we can read or hear most of these diverse voices and perspectives without stepping out of our own living room or leaving our favorite coffee shop. This is a border crossing of the mind and an opening up of the imagination.

There are blogs written by Americans who are DREAMers, DACA activists, first-generation immigrants, asylum seekers, undocumented journalists or actors, children of immigrants, and many others. They are all sharing the ways they navigate America. Read them. Listen to their voices and let your imagination draw you into their perspectives and their experience of the world. Do you prefer audio or video or the visual arts? There are TED talks, poetry readings, short documentaries, art installations, musical curations, and archives such as Alt-Latino,[5] IMM-Print,[6] Undocumented Voices,[7] and "Documenting the Undocumented"[8] that record and share immigrant voices through many forms of artistic expressions.[9] There are also more traditional resources that share insights and access to worldviews and experiences that take us out of our comfort zone. Films, documentaries, interviews, public murals, poetry, plays, and memoirs are ways you can enter into another person's worldview and experience. I have suggested resources below for further reading. But don't stop there. These are resources you can pick up and put down, share with friends, or add to a church library. Be sure to also get out and meet *people* where they live, dance, sing, act, build, serve, and work in your community.

Step 3: Meeting Immigrant Advocates and Leaders

A third step might be to bring in people who work with immigrants to speak with your congregation. Find out what you can do and connect with trustworthy organizations and the opportunities they have for volunteers. You might organize a panel for multiple congregations or a community leaders' gathering. You can find local experts online, through legal advocacy resources, through interviews in local newspapers, or through community and city colleges as well as universities. You can also look to local city colleges and universities for talks that are open to the public. By volunteering with Know Your Rights groups, voter registration drives, DACA renewal, or other programs that assist immigrants, you will hear stories from immigrants and their families in person. Consider, too, that many people living at the margins have few resources, work multiple jobs, and have many family responsibilities. Go to *them* to learn more, rather than taking them from their commitments to teach you. By going out into the community to serve or volunteer, you make more interactions across social boundaries possible. This benefits all of us and strengthens our community networks.

You have practiced being a guest and getting out of your comfort zone, your congregational borders, and your preferred cultural spaces. You have listened to, seen, and read from the voices, art, and perspectives created by immigrants, undocumented people, students, artists, journalists, and families navigating the US immigration system all across the US. You've learned from those who work with, support, and advocate for immigrants who seek asylum, face detention, or come from families divided by political borders—and others who have had to immigrate for different, complex reasons. And now you want to do more. There are many ways to get involved in supporting immigrants and refugees directly. These opportunities make up a fourth step.

Step 4: Becoming an Advocate, an Ally, an Educator

Advocate Politically for Immigration Reform

You can get involved with local or national political advocacy to change our inadequate and broken immigration system. Let your member of Congress know what is important to you. Vote for representatives who have laid out clear policies on reforming the immigration system and for addressing the refugee crises at the US-Mexico border. Ask your representatives and those running for local office what their position is on the use of for-profit detention centers, the institutionalization of detained families, and where the resources of food and medical care for asylum seekers will come from. Have a letter-writing party in your neighborhood, or have congregants write letters demanding federal action on immigration reform if they feel so led during a moment for mission. Find out what your denomination's position is on immigration and lead a workshop to help your local congregation or faith community engage and discuss that position.[10] Consider volunteering your time and talents to offer legal, medical, or tax assistance or other professional help to immigrants in your state.

There are local and national groups who offer different levels of training and resources for each of these kinds of supportive action. I particularly like Freedom for Immigrants, a national organization with a simple mission that I have mentioned throughout this book. They are committed to advocating for the release of detainees from incarceration facilities and to accompanying detainees through their process of detention, hearings, and release or deportation. Freedom for Immigrants has a clear and easily navigable website with a map of existing detention centers and prison facilities used by ICE. They manage the IMM-Print archive of stories, art, and poetry created by detainees to share with the public. And they have clearly outlined ways you can get involved at all levels, from political and legislative activism, to raising bond monies, to writing letters and visiting people in detention.

Becoming an ally of immigrant-led organizations is also a political act. There are many national, immigrant-led organizations you can support directly,[11] including the UndocuBlack Network.[12] Inaugurated in 2016, UndocuBlack is "a multigenerational network of currently and formerly undocumented Black people that fosters community, facilitates access to resources, and contributes to transforming the realities of our people, so we are thriving and living our fullest lives."[13]

Give Financial Support

Most organizations for the support of immigrants have ways you can give financially to benefit people in specific ways. These include legal funds, bond monies, and start-up funds for families recently granted asylum to establish their lives in the US. Families of detainees often lack gas money for visitation. Juvenile detainees often need clothes and food when they are released into the care of a sponsor, and those who are being deported after time in detention need a backpack and clothes to take with them when they leave for their country of birth. Many colleges and universities have set up educational funds that go to help DACA and DREAMer students pay for semester supplies, food, housing, or transportation to their classes. If you don't live near one of these schools, you and your church or community organization could start such a fund. Private funds and scholarships often make the difference between students having the books they need for their courses and not finishing a semester because they lack the materials.

Crowdfunding is also a good way to help. For example, Pueblo Sin Fronteras and Freedom for Immigrants are working together on a family reunification project in response to the numbers of children and parents who are being separated at the border.[14]

Offer Personal Advocacy and Direct Support

Rather than make a financial contribution, many people prefer to jump in and work directly with those in need. Many Americans are keenly aware of the children separated from their family members at the border and want to help these children. Al Otro Lado[15] is one nonprofit organization that is doing this work to support immigrants at the border. They have programs of support for volunteers on the ground, and they offer medical and legal advocacy, as well as family reunification services.[16]

Another is Pueblo Sin Fronteras,[17] a cross-border organization that has two shelters—one in Sonora, Mexico, and one in Tijuana. Their US shelters aim to support those in detention centers. Their mission "promotes accompaniment, humanitarian assistance, leadership development, recognition of human rights, and coordination of know-your-rights training along migrant routes, as well as monitoring and raising awareness of human rights abuses against migrants and refugees in Mexico and the United States."[18]

Another organization is the Sanctuary Movement.[19] This site has resources in Spanish and English, links to denominational resources, a "faith tool kit," and steps for how to start a local coalition or, using their map, find coalitions across the US that you can join.

The New Sanctuary Coalition[20] organizes accompaniment training in the New York area. This is a hands-on program that "recruits and trains volunteers to accompany people facing deportation to their immigration hearings and ICE check-ins. This provides moral support to the person facing deportation and enables volunteers to hold immigration authorities accountable."[21] They also have a web page offering resources and support to immigrants, especially in the New York area,[22] as well as an "allies and resources" page listing local and national immigration support groups.[23]

Accompanying our immigrant brothers and sisters in this way is not easy. It is often more frustrating than rewarding, and it can feel devastating when we are deeply committed to advocating for specific individuals and our advocacy doesn't end in the desired result. The work can also be time-consuming. That said, there are organizations with experience in accompaniment that offer training for those of us who want to get involved directly. Look for programs that organize detention center visits or that support or train sanctuary church, synagogue, and mosque congregations to receive an undocumented person with a deportation or removal order. There are also possibilities for accompanying minors through the court system or accompanying detainees to their ICE visits. More simply, through your public school system you can tutor immigrant children whose first language is not English.

And don't forget that organizations you already support may be doing work with immigrants and refugees. These include Habitat for Humanity, Clergy and Laity United for Economic Justice (CLUE), Catholic Charities, the National Organization for Women, and the American Civil Liberties Union. Check with your faith-based group for national and denominational resources that focus on immigrant rights and advocacy.[24]

Educate Your Community

The more people are involved in as many different ways as possible, the deeper the change will be in our communities as we open our hearts to our immigrant neighbors. Know that you don't have to invent a community fundraiser, activity, or curriculum. Many national organizations have step-by-step directions for fundraising or refugee kit assembly projects, as well as downloadable educational resources online for "know your rights" campaigns that you can implement, and online spaces for donation collection and distribution.

For example, the Sanctuary Movement of Church World Service, based in Washington, DC, offers a global approach to sanctuary movements,[25] immigration support, and resources for getting involved.[26] But they also have excellent educational resources and paths for involvement at all levels: financial giving programs; resources for organizing community events such as a CROP Walk; direct-involvement projects such as putting together refugee "kits" or welcoming a refugee into your neigh-borhood; as well as educational materials such as congrega-tional worship and group study handouts.

Additional sites with resources include the Immigrant De-fense Project in New York;[27] the Coalition for Humane Im-migration Rights (CHIRLA),[28] which posts accessible online educational films; Migra Map,[29] one of a number of mapping projects and texting alert systems that track ICE and immigra-tion raids; and Mariposas Sin Fronteras,[30] an organization that supports LGBTQ people in detention. The Immigrant Legal Resources Center[31] also has educational materials, a where-to-go-for-information page, and a focus on legal help.

Tell Your Story

Whatever your level of involvement, immigrants need to hear from people like you about what you have learned and how you want to help. To this end, writing an op-ed or story for your local paper, your alumni magazine, or your community or church bulletin is a way you can amplify awareness of what our immigrant neighbors are experiencing in the US. Certainly, sharing stories of your advocacy experiences in public can ex-pand your boundaries and invite others to listen. If writing or public speaking is not your style, speaking informally to your congregation, to a board you sit on, or to a knitting group or parents support group, or even mentioning in congrega-tional prayers the people you have met or the funds you have contributed to, is an additional way of broadening awareness and inviting more people to ask you about your experience. In telling your story, you lift up the stories of the immigrants and refugees whom you have met and come to care about. The people listening to you can then begin stepping out of their comfort zones at their own pace. Your story may help others open their hearts to the stories of their immigrant neighbors.

For Further Reading

Books That Explore Biblical Understanding and Immigration

Carroll R., M. Daniel. *The Bible and Borders: Hearing God's Word on Immigration.* Grand Rapids: Brazos, 2020.

Daniel, Ben. *Neighbor: Christian Encounters with "Illegal" Immigration.* Louisville: Westminster John Knox, 2010.

Myers, Ched, and Matthew Colwell. *Our God Is Undocumented: Biblical Faith and Immigrant Justice.* Maryknoll, NY: Orbis Books, 2012.

Nanko-Fernandez, Carmen. *Theologizing in Espanglish.* Maryknoll, NY: Orbis Books, 2010.

Books That Present Migrant, Immigrant, Asylum Seeker, and Undocumented Voices

Adichie, Chimamanda Ngozi. *Americanah.* New York: Knopf, 2013.

Davis, Joshua. *Spare Parts: Four Undocumented Teenagers, One Ugly Robot, and the Battle for the American Dream.* New York: Farrar, Straus & Giroux, 2014.

De La Torre, Miguel A. *Trails of Hope and Terror: Testimonies on Immigration.* Maryknoll, NY: Orbis Books, 2013.

Dumas, Firoozeh. *Funny in Farsi: A Memoir of Growing Up Iranian in America.* New York: Random House, 2004.

Fadiman, Anne. *The Spirit Catches You and You Fall Down: A Hmong Child, Her American Doctors, and the Collision of Two Cultures.* New York: Farrar, Straus & Giroux, 1997.

Foster, Patrice. *Left across the Border.* N.p.: patricemfoster.com, 2016.

Guerrero, Diane. *In the Country We Love: My Family Divided.* New York: St. Martin's Griffin, 2017.

Iyer, Deepa. *We Too Sing America: South Asian, Arab, Muslim, and Sikh Immigrants Shape Our Multiracial Future.* New York: The New Press, 2015.

Michelson, Seth, ed. *Dreaming America: Voices of Undocumented Youth in Maximum Security Detention.* Silver Spring, MD: Settlement House, 2017.

Navejas, José Ángel. *Illegal: Reflections of an Undocumented Immigrant.* Urbana: University of Illinois Press, 2014.

Nazario, Sonia. *Enrique's Journey: The Story of a Boy's Dangerous Odyssey to Reunite with His Mother.* New York: Random House, 2014.

Orner, Peter, ed. *Underground America: Narratives of Undocumented Lives.* Brooklyn, NY: Verso, 2017.

Pérez, William. *We Are Americans: Undocumented Students Pursuing the American Dream.* Sterling, VA: Stylus, 2009.

Pope Francis. *A Stranger and You Welcomed Me: A Call to Mercy and Solidarity with Migrants and Refugees.* Edited by Robert Ellsberg. Maryknoll, NY: Orbis Books, 2018.

Tonatiuh, Duncan. *Undocumented: A Worker's Fight.* New York: Abrams ComicArts, 2018.

Vargas, Jose Antonio. *Dear America: Notes of an Undocumented Citizen.* New York: Harper Luxe, 2018.

Books That Offer Historical and Political Perspectives on Immigration in the US and Globally

Castles, Stephen, Hein de Hass, and Mark J. Miller. *The Age of Migration: International Population Movements in the Modern World.* 5th ed. New York: The Guilford Press, 2014.

Chomsky, Aviva. *Undocumented: How Immigration Became Illegal.* Boston: Beacon Press, 2014.

Gonzalez, Juan. *Harvest of Empire: A History of Latinos in America.* Rev. ed. New York: Penguin Books, 2011.

Olmsted, Kathryn S. *Right Out of California: The 1930s and the Big Business Roots of Modern Conservatism.* New York: The New Press, 2017.

Guides to Personal and Congregational Involvement

Brazal, Agnes M., and María Theresa Dávila, eds. *Living with(out) Borders: Catholic Theological Ethics on the Migrations of Peoples.* Catholic Theological Ethics in the World Church 4. Maryknoll, NY: Orbis Books, 2016.

Carroll R., M. Daniel. *Christians at the Border: Immigration, the Church, and the Bible.* 2nd ed. Grand Rapids: Brazos, 2013.

Fogg, Julia Lambert. "Immigration, Migration, and Border Crossing: Scenarios from the College Classroom." In *Global Lutheranism: Vitality and Challenges,* edited by Peter Vethanayagamony, F. Volker Greifenhagen, and Association of Teaching Theologians, 207–31. Minneapolis: Lutheran University Press, 2018.

Morris, Rosalind C., ed. *Can the Subaltern Speak? Reflections on an Idea.* New York: Columbia University Press, 2010.

Salvatierra, Alexia, and Peter Heltzel. *Faith-Rooted Organizing: Mobilizing the Church in Service to the World.* Downers Grove, IL: Inter-Varsity, 2014.

Notes

Chapter 1 Walk This Way: Approaching the Border

1. My ancestors were European colonists from various places—England, Ireland, and Germany, among others. This means that I am a settler on lands that did not belong to them or to me. I do not take up the question of justice for Native Americans or First Nations peoples in this book, but I do want to acknowledge my debt to the people who have lived in the Americas before European settlers inscribed colonial borders and took their lands.

2. I discuss how I apply this work pedagogically in "Immigration, Migration, and Border Crossing: Scenarios from the College Classroom," in *Global Lutheranism: Vitality and Challenges*, ed. Peter Vethanayagamony and F. Volker Greifenhagen (Minneapolis: Lutheran University Press, 2018), 207–31.

3. Lori Robertson, "The DACA Population Numbers," FactCheck, January 12, 2018, https://www.factcheck.org/2018/01/daca-population-numbers/.

4. Michael D. Shear and Adam Liptak, "It's Now the Supreme Court's Turn to Try to Resolve the Fate of the DREAMers," *New York Times*, June 28, 2019, https://www.nytimes.com/2019/06/28/us/politics/supreme-court-daca-dreamers.html.

5. For example, M. Eugene Boring characterizes Matthew's interpretation of the exodus narrative this way: "Jesus is pictured as fulfilling in his own experience the story of Israel." Boring, "The Gospel of Matthew," in *The New Interpreter's Bible*, ed. Leander E. Keck (Nashville: Abingdon, 1995), 8:146.

6. In 2:15, Matthew is interpreting Hosea 11:1–2: "When Israel was a child, I loved him, / and out of Egypt I called my son. / The more I called them, / the more they went from me." The prophet Hosea uses "son" as a collective noun referring to the whole people, the Israelites in Egypt. Matthew, however, applies this collective noun to a singular person, Jesus. This quotation exemplifies Matthew's presentation of Jesus's childhood events merged with the exodus story of Jesus's ancestors. I develop this connection further in chap. 2.

7. "In a worship service opening the Churches against Racism conference in Doorn, Netherlands, 14–17 June, World Council of Churches (WCC) general secretary Rev. Dr. Samuel Kobia said the Bible was the 'ultimate immigration handbook.'" "Bible Is the 'Ultimate Immigration Handbook,'" World Council of Churches, June 15, 2009, https://www.oikoumene.org/en/press-centre/news/bible-is-the-ultimate-immigration-handbook. For a more recent discussion of reading the New Testament as stories of migrants and migration, see, e.g., Margaret Aymer, "Rootlessness and Community in Contexts of Diaspora," in *Fortress Commentary on the Bible: The New Testament*, ed. Margaret Aymer, Cynthia Briggs Kittredge, and David A. Sánchez (Minneapolis: Fortress, 2014), 47–61.

8. The approach of listening to people who are marginalized by unjust systems of political, social, and economic power is growing in biblical interpretation. One direction this approach takes, e.g., is Richard Horsley's edited volume *Christian Origins*, vol. 1 of *A People's History of Christianity* (Minneapolis: Augsburg Fortress, 2006). Another is the multivolume Wisdom Commentary series edited by Barbara Reid (Liturgical Press). See also *True to Our Native Land: An African American New Testament Commentary*, ed. Brian K. Blount (Minneapolis: Fortress, 2007).

9. Although the focus of this work is on selections from the Gospels and Pauline letters, I do also look briefly at Ruth. Other scholars have done more extensive work on Ruth. See, e.g., César Melgar's "Ruth and the Unaccompanied Minors from Central America: Ethical Perspectives on a Socio-Economic Problem," *Review & Expositor* 112, no. 2 (May 2015): 269–79; M. Daniel Carroll R., "Once a Stranger, Always a Stranger? Immigration, Assimilation, and the Book of Ruth," *International Bulletin of Missionary Research* 39, no. 4 (October 2015): 185–88. On the themes of "sojourner" and "alien" in the Old Testament, see, e.g., Donald E. Gowan, "Wealth and Poverty in the Old Testament: The Case for the Widow, Orphan, and Sojourner," *Interpretation* 41, no. 4 (October 1987): 341–53; and Joseph R. Kelly, "The Ethics of Inclusion: The *gr* and the *'zrh* in the Passover to YHWH," *Bulletin for Biblical Research* 23, no. 2 (2013): 155–66.

10. David Masci and Gregory A. Smith, "5 Facts about U.S. Evangelical Protestants," FactTank, Pew Research Center, March 1, 2018, https://www.pewresearch.org/fact-tank/2018/03/01/5-facts-about-u-s-evangelical-protestants/.

11. "About every five hundred years the empowered structures of institutionalized Christianity, whatever they may be at that time, become an intolerable carapace that must be shattered in order that renewal and new growth may occur." Phyllis Tickle, *The Great Emergence: How Christianity Is Changing and Why* (Grand Rapids: Baker Books, 2008), 16.

Chapter 2 Fleeing without Papers

1. All names have been changed and identifying details changed or omitted. The people are real, but their stories are told from my perspective and

interactions with them. The exception is Hugo's story in chapter 5. I have not met Hugo, and all of the details of his story come from publicly accessed publications.

2. See Roberto G. Gonzales, "Learning to Be Illegal: Undocumented Youth and Shifting Legal Contexts in the Transition to Adulthood," *American Sociological Review* 76, no. 4 (2011): 602–19.

3. Compare the experience of Eboo Patel in *Acts of Faith: The Story of an American Muslim, the Struggle for the Soul of a Generation* (Boston: Beacon, 2007). Patel argues that it is precisely such early adult mentoring and interest in a young person that can make the difference between a child who turns to violence (against themselves or others) and a child who turns to constructive community contributions.

4. Many undocumented teens discover their legal status suddenly and without preparation, often around age sixteen, when they want to learn to drive. Many times even their families do not completely understand the complex legal processes and ramifications of living without documentation. Other students start on the college track with their friends in high school and then discover that college is out of the question because they do not have Social Security numbers to enter on college applications. Even though there are alternative ways to apply, the initial impact is devastating. They can feel completely alone, imagining they are the only undocumented one in their family, their class, their neighborhood. Many of these students find their way forward through activism. They become "DREAMers" (young people who would qualify for the federal Development, Relief and Education for Alien Minors Act if it were passed) and embrace their American upbringing as well as their parental heritage. They claim a future for themselves by organizing. They help each other; they study law and organize fundraisers to be able to afford tuition and books for college. They win private scholarships to four-year institutions. They become, in other words, deeply invested and committed to furthering the American promises they grew up believing.

Journalist Jose Antonio Vargas is perhaps one of the most well-known DREAMers in the US. His story "My Life as an Undocumented Immigrant" was first published in the *New York Times* on June 22, 2011. See https://www.ny times.com/2011/06/26/magazine/my-life-as-an-undocumented-immigrant.html.

5. For this history, see, e.g., John M. G. Barclay's *Jews in the Mediterranean Diaspora: From Alexander to Trajan (323 BCE–117 CE)* (Berkeley: University of California Press, 1996; rev. ed., London: Bloomsbury T&T Clark, 2015).

6. Luke places Mary and Joseph's hometown in Nazareth (Luke 1:26–27) and has them travel to Bethlehem for a census. Matthew tells the birth narrative differently, placing the couple in Bethlehem for Jesus's birth. Later, after they flee Bethlehem for Egypt, they return north, and Nazareth becomes their eventual home. I follow Matthew's narrative here. But whether Mary is originally from Nazareth or Bethlehem, as a refugee in Egypt she would be without her nearest kin.

7. Sometime after Santiago turned thirty, his mother found a small photo of him as a baby in his father's arms. The photo had been taken in Mexico. That is the first time he remembers seeing his father's face.

8. On foot, the most direct route today from Chihuahua, Mexico, to San Diego, California, is about 900 miles. The holy family's walk from Bethlehem to, for example, Alexandria, Egypt, would have been about 600–700 miles. Today, children and families are fleeing even farther—about 3,000 miles from Nicaragua, Guatemala, or Honduras to San Diego or Los Angeles.

9. The distinction between "migrant" and "immigrant" is one of degree or specificity. An immigrant is someone who moves from one country (or politically bounded rule) to another. "Migrant" is a more general term referring to one who moves from one place to another. Under the first-century Roman Empire, there were no countries, but there were regional rulers like Herod the Great, whose command ended at specific borders. Defined this way, Jesus's family "migrated" within the Roman Empire, but they "immigrated" from one kingdom (Herod's rule of Judea) to another (the Ptolemaic) kingdom.

10. For example, M. Eugene Boring characterizes Matthew's interpretation of the exodus narrative this way: "Jesus is pictured as fulfilling in his own experience the story of Israel." Boring, "The Gospel of Matthew," in *The New Interpreter's Bible*, ed. Leander E. Keck (Nashville: Abingdon, 1995), 8:146.

11. Boring, "The Gospel of Matthew," 8:146.

12. See, e.g., Warren Carter, "Matthew," in *Fortress Commentary on the Bible: The New Testament*, ed. Margaret Aymer, Cynthia Briggs Kittredge, and David A. Sánchez (Minneapolis: Fortress, 2014), 133–34.

13. See, e.g., Luke Timothy Johnson, *The Writings of the New Testament: An Interpretation* (Minneapolis: Fortress, 1999), 194.

14. See Julia Chavarría's visual interpretation of Matt. 2:16 entitled *The Slaughter of the Innocents*. Her work renders the first-century moment in the iconography of the Nicaraguan war. See *The Gospel in Art by the Peasants of Solentiname*, ed. Philip Scharper and Sally Scharper (Maryknoll, NY: Orbis Books, 1984), 19.

15. Ekkehard W. Stegemann and Wolfgang Stegemann, *The Jesus Movement: A Social History of Its First Century*, trans. O. C. Dean Jr. (Minneapolis: Fortress, 1995), 49. Warren Carter does not mention "conscription," but otherwise describes the deprivations and suffering of Jews in the first century under Roman taxation and Herod's economic programs. These programs moved wealth from the rural areas of Palestine to the wealthy living in a few urban pockets. See Carter, "Matthew's People," in *Christian Origins*, vol. 1 of *A People's History of Christianity*, ed. Richard Horsley (Minneapolis: Augsburg Fortress, 2010), 138–61. For a deep dive into the economic policies of the Herodians, see Douglas E. Oakman, "Power and Imperium," in *The Political Aims of Jesus* (Minneapolis: Fortress, 2012), 45–78.

16. Barry J. Beitzel writes that "Herod became almost obsessed with founding/rebuilding cities in fine Roman style, and with constructing theaters, amphitheaters, hippodromes, temples, fortresses, aqueducts, gymnasia, and

palaces throughout Palestine. . . . He also undertook to erect the Temple in Jerusalem in magnificent fashion. Begun in 20 BC and completed in AD 63, just seven years before its demolition, this project required the labor of 10,000 men for ten years, just to fashion the retaining walls around the Temple platform." See Beitzel, "Herod the Great: Another Snapshot of His Treachery?" *Journal of the Evangelical Theological Society* 57, no. 2 (2014): 311.

17. Philip L. Martin, Michael Fix, and J. Edward Taylor, *The New Rural Poverty: Agriculture and Immigration in California* (Washington, DC: Urban Institute Press, 2006).

18. For example, Valeria Ramirez, "Behind the Fields: The Importance of the Bandana Project," University of Idaho Women's Center, March 30, 2017, https://uiwomenscenter.wordpress.com/2017/03/30/behind-the-feilds -the-importance-of-the-bandana-project/.

19. For example, to learn about the Mixtec community in Ventura County, California, see "Mixtecs in Ventura County," Mixteco, http://mixteco.org /mixtecs/.

20. "The list of Herod's executions of family members include three of his sons, his Hasmonean wife Mariamne, and his wife's mother and grandfather." See Morten Hørning Jensen, "Herod the Great," Bible Odyssey, https://www.bibleodyssey.org/people/main-articles/herod-the-great.

21. "Knowing the Jewish aversion to pork, it is reported that Augustus, on hearing of Herod's execution of his own son Antipater, made the pun that he would rather be Herod's pig (Greek: ὑς) than Herod's son (υἱος)." Isaiah Gafni, "Augustus (63 B.C.E.–14 C.E.)," Jewish Virtual Library, https://www .jewishvirtuallibrary.org/augustus.

22. Sonia Nazario, *Enrique's Journey: The Story of a Boy's Dangerous Odyssey to Reunite with His Mother* (New York: Random House, 2014).

23. Julia Ainsley and Courtney Kube, "Hundreds of Migrant Kids Separated from Parents Are Stuck at Border Stations," NBC News, June 5, 2018, https://www.nbcnews.com/news/us-news/hundreds-migrant-kids-separated -parents-are-stuck-border-stations-n878696.

24. "DREAMers" are young people who would qualify for the federal Development, Relief and Education for Alien Minors Act if it were passed.

25. Jonathan Reed, "Life in First Century Galilee," Bible Odyssey, video, 3:59, https://www.bibleodyssey.org/en/tools/video-gallery/l/life-in-first-century -galilee; and Richard A. Horsley presents a view of Galilee as a home of thieves ("Josephus and the Bandits," *Journal for the Study of Judaism* 10, no. 1 [1979]: 37–63), but there have since been other reconstructions. See also Bradley W. Root, *First Century Galilee: A Fresh Examination of the Sources* (Tübingen: Mohr Siebeck, 2014). Root offers a critical examination of historical reconstructions of first-century Galilee.

26. Chris Keith, "Jesus and Literacy," Bible Odyssey, https://www.bible odyssey.org/en/tools/ask-a-scholar/jesus-and-literacy.

27. "Code-switching" is a term used by linguists to describe how people move in conversation between one language, or set of linguistic codes, and

another. For example, see Gene Demby, "How Code-Switching Explains the World," *Code Switch: Race and Identity Remix*, April 8, 2013, https://www .npr.org/blogs/codeswitch/2013/04/08/176064688/how-code-switching-exp lains-the-world.

28. DACA was an executive order signed by President Obama in 2012. It offered not citizenship but rather a two-year renewable status that included the possibility of a work permit and driver's license for immigrants who arrived in the US as children. In 2014, President Obama announced DAPA, an expansion of DACA offered to parents of American citizens on a three-year renewable basis. Court decisions kept DAPA from going into effect. In California, Assembly Bill 540 was signed in 2001 by Governor Gray Davis and became part of the California Education Code. This bill allows students who are not legal residents, but who have attended high school in California for three years or more and have received a diploma, to attend colleges in California at the state's residential tuition rate.

Chapter 3 Vantage Points and Borders—Where We Stand Shapes How We See

1. For example, see Raúl Homero Villa and George Sanchez, eds., *Los Angeles and the Future of Urban Cultures: A Special Issue of the American Quarterly* (Baltimore: Johns Hopkins University Press, 2005).

2. Many seminaries recognize this lacuna. Seminaries and theological schools are developing programs to shape pastoral and congregational leaders not just for cultural sensitivity but, more importantly, for cultural agility and asset-based perspectives on engaging diverse identities. One such program is TEEM (Theological Education for Emerging Ministries), a collaboration of Pacific Lutheran Theological Seminary (PLTS) at California Lutheran University with Luther Seminary, Lutheran Center in Atlanta, and the Church Divinity School of the Pacific, all schools of the Evangelical Lutheran Church in America. I am most familiar with the program I teach in, directed by Rev. Dr. Moses Penumaka at PLTS in Berkeley, California, https://www.plts.edu /programs/certificates/teem.html.

3. It is vital to remember that all communities—from the most well-endowed to the most downtrodden—have gifts, strengths, and resources. When pastors and community leaders come into a neighborhood or church to "help," we must start by listening to the neighbors and faith members, hearing their inventory of community assets so that we begin from their re-sources rather than importing solutions from outside. For an understanding of an asset-based (asking what resources communities have) rather than a deficit-based (starting with what communities lack) approach, see John Mc-Knight and John Kretzman's Asset-Based Community Development (ABCD) Institute, https://resources.depaul.edu/abcd-institute/about/Pages/default .aspx. Carl S. Dudley and Nancy T. Ammerman have adapted McKnight and Kretzman's work for congregations in *Congregations in Transition: A*

Guide for Analyzing, Assessing, and Adapting in Changing Communities (San Francisco: Jossey-Bass, 2002).

4. Stephen C. Barton, "Why Do Things Move People? The Jerusalem Temple as Emotional Repository," *Journal for the Study of the New Testament* 37, no. 4 (June 2015): 367. Barton describes the holy character of the temple conveyed through, among other things, the architecture of the courtyards: "This temple holiness was communicated by means of a profound symbolic system of purity rules worked out in overlapping and mutually reinforcing separations, distinctions, discriminations and even elevations. In its spatial aspect, its application and practice were oriented on symbolic intensification. In ever-decreasing circles, the purity system covered the land of Israel, the city of Jerusalem and the temple, with ever-tightening circles within the temple itself."

5. "Architecturally, the temple was ordered in terms of a sequence of clearly demarcated courts, leading, in ascending height and degree of holiness, from the outer Court of the Gentiles, to the Court of the Women, to the Court of the (ordinary male) Israelites, to the Court of the Priests, and finally to the sanctuary, itself divided between the first chamber (with incense altar and candelabrum) and the Holy of Holies. The ritual and moral seriousness of this sequence of separations cannot be underestimated. They express the holiness of God and the holiness of the people of God." Barton, "Why Do Things Move People?," 367.

6. See Eric M. Meyers and Mark A. Chancey, *Alexander to Constantine*, vol. 3 of *Archaeology of the Land of the Bible* (New Haven: Yale University Press, 2012), 58: "No foreigner is to enter within the forecourt and the balustrade around the sanctuary. Whoever is caught will have himself to blame for his subsequent death." E. P. Sanders also discusses the temple in chapter 6 of *Judaism: Practice and Belief, 63 BCE–66 CE* (London: SCM, 1992).

7. Mark and Matthew, in contrast to Luke and John, have Jesus enter Jerusalem only once, in Jesus's final week of ministry. In the Gospel of John, Jesus celebrates multiple festivals in Jerusalem (2:13; 5:1; 12:12), while in Luke, Jesus accompanies his family to Jerusalem multiple times (2:22, 42).

8. Jesus's act seems to have been a protest about the economic corruption of the temple being at odds with the temple serving as a place of prayer "for all the nations" (Mark 11:17).

9. Mark uses the imperfect in 11:17 to describe Jesus's actions: "He was teaching and he was saying to them . . ."

Chapter 4 Challenging Border Wall Mentalities

1. For example, Marianne B. Kartzow and Halvor Moxnes outline the importance of an intersectional identity approach using Acts 8. See Kartzow and Moxnes, "Complex Identities: Ethnicity, Gender and Religion in the Story of the Ethiopian Eunuch (Acts 8:26–40)," *Religion and Theology* 17 (2010): 184–204.

2. Churches in the Holiness tradition began ordaining women in the 1800s, including the Methodist Church in 1866. Mainline Protestant denominations like the Presbyterian Church USA began ordaining women to ministry in 1956; the Evangelical Lutheran Church in America followed in 1970, and Episcopalians in 1977. Jewish rabbis were also ordained along similar time-lines. See "Timeline of Women's Ordination in the United States," Wikipedia, https://en.wikipedia.org/wiki/Timeline_of_women%27s_ordination _in_the_United_States (last updated November 6, 2019). A recent book on the subject is Benjamin Knoll and Cammie Jo Bolin, *She Preached the Word: Women's Ordination in Modern America* (New York: Oxford University Press, 2018).

3. For an excellent, detailed history of migration and labor trends, see Juan Gonzalez, *Harvest of Empire: A History of Latinos in America*, rev. ed. (New York: Penguin, 2011). A DVD version of *Harvest of Empire* is also available from Onyx Films. For shorter, documentary-style films about conditions on the ground, see Emmy Award–winning journalist John Carlos Frey's works, such as *The Invisible Mexicans of Deer Canyon* (Los Angeles: Gatekeeper Productions, 2006), 73 min.

4. For an example of the "push factors"—the circumstances at home that influence a migrant's decision to leave—see the documentary film *Mojados: Through the Night* (Vanguard Cinema, 2005).

5. Around the same time that Trump came into office, the number of refugees from Guatemala, Nicaragua, El Salvador, and Honduras began to increase. These Central American families suffered from hunger, chronic states of war, gangs, and other political and economic violence. The Trump administration threatened the caravans of refugees. Due process for asylum seekers slowed to a crawl, families were separated, detention centers were overrun, and children were "lost" to their parents in the process. The crisis only worsens. Reihan Salam offers an analysis of the caravan crisis that began in Honduras: "The Solution to the Caravan Crisis Is in Honduras," *The Atlantic*, October 24, 2018, https://www.theatlantic.com/ideas/archive/201 8/10/solution-caravan-crisis-honduras/573832/.

The Pew Research Center offers interactive maps with nonpartisan immigration data as well as data analysis on immigration trends on their website. See their "Unauthorized Immigrant Population Trends for States, Birth Countries and Regions," https://www.pewresearch.org/hispanic/interactives /unauthorized-trends/.

6. In this chapter, because I am telling the story of women at a symposium, I focus on the experiences of mothers throughout. Undocumented fathers experience similar fears and pressures and must also find ways to secure their children's futures against their possible deportation. For example, see *A Better Life*, directed by Chris Weitz (Summit Entertainment, 2011).

7. The Center for Immigration Studies maps "sanctuary jurisdictions" across the US. It defines sanctuary jurisdictions as "cities, counties, and states [that] have laws, ordinances, regulations, resolutions, policies, or other

practices that obstruct immigration enforcement and shield criminals [*sic*] from ICE—either by refusing to or prohibiting agencies from complying with ICE detainers, imposing unreasonable conditions on detainer acceptance, denying ICE access to interview incarcerated aliens, or otherwise impeding communication or information exchanges between their personnel and federal immigration officers." See Bryan Griffith and Jessica M. Vaughan, "Map: Sanctuary Cities, Counties, and States," April 16, 2019, https://cis .org/Map-Sanctuary-Cities-Counties-and-States.

8. In this way, we continue the work Matthew began in his Gospel to interpret Jewish Scriptures, such as the story of the exodus, through Jesus's life when we interpret biblical stories through the lives of underrepresented women and immigrants (see chap. 2).

9. Many have written on the book of Ruth and contemporary immigration. See, e.g., M. Daniel Carroll R., "Once a Stranger, Always a Stranger? Immigration, Assimilation, and the Book of Ruth," *International Bulletin of Missionary Research* (October 1, 2015): 185–88; and Bonnie Honig, "The Foreigner as Immigrant," in *Democracy and the Foreigner* (Princeton: Princeton University Press, 2001), 41–72.

10. There are many resources for exploring linkages in global and local economies. Many look at how the pull of economies in one region increases or decreases the push of local economies in another region. For example, see Pamela Brubaker, Rebecca Todd Peters, and Laura Stivers, eds., *Justice in a Global Economy: Strategies for Home, Community, and World* (Louisville: Westminster John Knox, 2006).

11. See "Projects," Alianza Nacional de Campesinas, https://www.alianza nacionaldecampesinas.org/projects, as well as PBS Frontline's interview with Dolores Huerta by Jason Breslow, "Dolores Huerta: An 'Epidemic in the Fields'" (June 25, 2013), https://www.pbs.org/wgbh/frontline/article/dolores -huerta-an-epidemic-in-the-fields/.

12. In fact, this is how the mother of one of my students tells her story. When she crossed the US-Mexico border alone twenty years ago, she too "covenanted" with another woman traveling alone. They promised they would not leave each other as they made their way across a river and a desert in a group of male strangers. Their covenant was tested, but they managed to keep each other awake, safe, and moving through the physical pain they experienced until they arrived in the US. My thanks to A., CLU class of 2022.

13. Amy Chua, *Political Tribes: Group Instinct and the Fate of Nations* (New York: Penguin, 2018), 1.

14. Jesus has a similar effect on the fishermen who become his first disciples. They "immediately" drop their nets to follow him (Mark 1:18–20). And the Gerasene demoniac who "immediately" (5:2) runs to meet Jesus wants to follow him (5:18). So when the Syrophoenician woman "immediately" hears about Jesus and comes and "bows down at his feet" (7:25), it is clear that she too is poised to become a follower of Jesus.

15. There are those who argue that Jesus's words are not derogatory. Rebekah Liu, for example, tries to make the case that the Greek word Jesus uses, "little dog," should be taken to refer to "household pets" rather than to stray "dogs" and thus "reveals his tender feelings, betraying his love for this Gentile woman." Liu, "A Dog under the Table at the Messianic Banquet: A Study of Mark 7:24–30," *Andrews University Seminary Studies* 48, no. 2 (2010): 251–55, here 254.

16. I agree with Jane Hicks that "Jesus' remark is most certainly insulting" ("Moral Agency at the Borders: Rereading the Story of the Syrophoenician Woman," *Word and World* 25, no. 1 [2003]: 81). In a much-cited chapter, Sharon Ringe describes Jesus's words as "flippant, even cruel, defying justification." Ringe, "A Gentile Woman's Story," in *Feminist Interpretation of the Bible*, ed. Letty M. Russell (Philadelphia: Westminster, 1985), 65–72, here 69.

17. In Matt. 15:28 Jesus declares, "Great is your faith!" and clearly heals the daughter in response: "and her daughter was healed instantly." There are many differences between the Matthean version of this story with a Canaanite mother, and the Markan version with a Syrophoenician mother. The way Matthew tells the story, Jesus and his disciples leave familiar Jewish territory around the Sea of Galilee and head northwest toward the coast "to the district of Tyre and Sidon," which is Gentile territory (Matt. 15:21). As they are passing through a town, a Canaanite woman begins to follow them. Canaanites and Jews were historical enemies. Still, the woman begs Jesus to heal her daughter, who is possessed by a demon: "Have mercy on me, Lord, Son of David; my daughter is tormented by a demon" (15:22). Jesus ignores the woman and does not answer. The disciples, however, can't ignore her. They turn to Jesus and urge him to "send her away, for she keeps shouting after us" (15:23). One can sympathize with their agitation. They are in unfamiliar territory, and it is a bit awkward for a group of Jewish men to arrive in a Canaanite town and have a woman following them along a public road, shouting and drawing attention to their small band. Just ignoring the woman will not work. The disciples want Jesus to respond.

When Jesus does respond, it is not clear if he is speaking to his disciples or to the woman. He draws a border around his ministry, saying, "I was sent only to the lost sheep of the house of Israel" (Matt. 15:24). This warning reminds the woman of their ethnic differences. Will a Canaanite dare to cross that line? The woman meets his challenge and kneels before Jesus, saying, "Lord, help me" (15:25). Jesus tests her again: "It is not fair to take the children's food and throw it to the dogs" (15:26). The Canaanite responds, "Yes, Lord, yet even the dogs eat the crumbs that fall from their masters' table" (15:27). Then Jesus publicly declares, "Woman, great is your faith! Let it be done for you as you wish" (15:28). With these words, Matthew reveals that Jesus set the ethnic boundaries as a test of faith. The Canaanite has passed! She receives her reward. Her daughter is healed as she wished.

But in Mark 7:24–30 Jesus does not mention the Syrophoenician woman's faith. It also appears that he does not heal the daughter, at least not explicitly.

There is no healing formula, and Jesus does not expel the demon. He simply observes that the demon is gone: "The demon has left your daughter" (7:29).

18. Two important works in this regard are Gerd Theissen's *The Gospels in Context: Social and Political History in the Synoptic Tradition*, trans. Linda M. Maloney (London: T&T Clark, 1992), and David Rhoads's narrative analysis, "Jesus and the Syrophoenician Woman in Mark: A Narrative Critical Study," *Journal of the American Academy of Religion* 62, no. 2 (Summer 1994): 343–75.

19. There are a number of politicians who have been caught on tape or in print referring to immigrants as "dogs." See, e.g., "Iowa's King Compares Immigrants to Dogs," *The Atlantic*, May 23, 2012, https://www.theatlantic.com /politics/archive/2012/05/iowas-king-compares-immigrants-to-dogs/427521/. For an analysis of President Trump's use of the term "dog" to refer to women, opponents, gang members, and immigrants, see Philip Bump's *Washington Post* article "Trump's Rationalization for Calling Women 'Dogs' Helped Define His Campaign," August 14, 2018, https://www.washingtonpost.com /news/politics/wp/2018/08/14/trumps-rationalization-for-calling-women -dogs-helped-define-his-campaign/?noredirect=on&utm_term=.0a866bdabbaf.

20. Jane Hicks makes the economic oppression of the Jews a cornerstone of her compelling reading of the Syrophoenician woman in Mark. She argues that if the woman was a member of the "urban elite" whose wealth came from oppressed Jews in Galilee, then "Jesus' household metaphor in which the bread goes first to the children of Israel would be understood by early listeners as a reversal in the reigning order" ("Moral Agency at the Borders," 82). See also Theissen, *Gospels in Context*, 72–77.

21. In Mark's Gospel, for example, Jesus ministers to crowds of people in 1:39, 45; 2:1–2; 3:7–12; 4:1; and 5:21, 31. He also travels to solitary places to rest in 3:19b–20; 6:31; and 6:53–56.

22. Raj Nadella makes a similar point, arguing that the Syrophoenician woman broadens the economic vision portrayed in the story: "In her articulation of this new economic vision, both the dogs and the children can enjoy a meal." Nadella, "The Two Banquets: Mark's Vision of Anti-Imperial Economics," *Interpretation* 70, no. 2 (2016): 172–83, here 178.

23. Jane Hicks calls this an increase in moral capacity: "Moral capacity is creatively realized in and through conversations across ethnic-cultural, economic and gender lines, where these borders indicate a real base in the lived world." Hicks, "Moral Agency at the Borders," 84.

Chapter 5 Letters from Behind Prison Walls

1. This is according to Bryan Baker, "Estimates of the Unauthorized Immigrant Population Residing in the United States: January 2014," Department of Homeland Security, July 2017, https://www.dhs.gov/sites/default/files /publications/Unauthorized%20Immigrant%20Population%20Estimates%2 0in%20the%20US%20January%202014_1.pdf.

2. I am using Hugo's real name because the sources I use for his story are all public. See Hugo Mejia, interview by Cindy Knoebel, "Here, It's All Concrete—Walls and Floors. We Never Get to See Outside, the Sun, Grass or Anything," IMM Print, October 17, 2017, https://imm-print.com/here-its -all-concrete-walls-and-floors-we-never-get-to-see-outside-the-sun-grass-or -anything/. Hugo's story is hosted by Freedom for Immigrants and protected under the Creative Commons license: https://creativecommons.org/licenses /by-nc-nd/4.0/.

3. For ICE statistics, see Immigration and Customs Enforcement, https:// www.ice.gov/features/ERO-2018. Undocumented residents in the US have not necessarily committed a federal crime. Entering the US without documenta- tion is a federal misdemeanor, and the response is deportation. Once someone has received "final orders" for deportation, however, and they reenter the US without permission, that reentry is now a "federal offense." See Laura Jarrett, "Are Undocumented Immigrants Committing a Crime? Not Necessarily," CNN Politics, February 24, 2017, https://www.cnn.com/2017/02/24/politics /undocumented-immigrants-not-necessarily-criminal/index.html.

4. Tatiana Sanchez, "Construction Worker Detained by ICE at Travis Air Force Base May Be Released for Thanksgiving," *The Mercury News*, Novem- ber 21, 2017, https://www.mercurynews.com/2017/11/21/construction-worker -detained-by-ice-on-travis-air-force-base-may-be-released-for-thanksgiving/.

5. Mejia, "Here, It's All Concrete."

6. Mejia, "Here, It's All Concrete."

7. Mejia, "Here, It's All Concrete."

8. Mejia, "Here, It's All Concrete."

9. Mejia, "Here, It's All Concrete."

10. Mejia, "Here, It's All Concrete."

11. Mejia, "Here, It's All Concrete."

12. Mejia, "Here, It's All Concrete."

13. Paul reminds the Corinthian churches, "If one member suffers, all suffer together with it; if one member is honored, all rejoice together with it" (1 Cor. 12:26).

14. Mejia, "Here, It's All Concrete."

15. Mejia, "Here, It's All Concrete."

16. See also Madison Pauly, "Washington Just Sued a Giant Private Prison Company for Paying Immigrant Workers $1 Per Day," *Mother Jones*, Sep- tember 20, 2017, https://www.motherjones.com/politics/2017/09/washington -just-sued-a-giant-private-prison-company-for-paying-immigrant-workers-1 -per-day/; and Jacqueline Stevens, "When Migrants Are Treated like Slaves," *New York Times*, April 4, 2018, https://www.nytimes.com/2018/04/04/opinion /migrants-detention-forced-labor.html. Others argue that the 2018 real cost per detainee is $208; see Laurence Benenson, "The Math of Immigration Detention, 2018 Update: Costs Continue to Multiply," May 9, 2018, https:// immigrationforum.org/article/math-immigration-detention-2018-update -costs-continue-mulitply/. These prices are skyrocketing for children at the

border in 2019, writes Luke Darby in "Trump's Child Detention Camps Cost $775 per Person Every Day," *GQ*, June 25, 2019, https://www.gq.com/story /trump-detention-camps-cost.

17. I have heard this anecdotally from multiple detainees and those who visit detainees. See also Gene Johnson, "GEO Group Seeks Dismissal of Lawsuit over Detainee Pay," *U.S. News*, November 20, 2017, https://www.us news.com/news/best-states/washington/articles/2017-11-20/geo-group-seeks -dismissal-of-lawsuit-over-detainee-pay; and Kieran Nicholson, "Immigrants Can Sue Federal Detention Center in Colorado over Forced Labor, Appeals Court Says," *Denver Post*, February 10, 2018, https://www.denverpost.com /2018/02/09/geo-group-aurora-immigration-detention-center-lawsuit/.

18. The GEO Group website states, "As more and more government agencies look to the private sector, we'll be hiring professionals like you to meet the demand. GEO's diversified range of services includes correctional and detention operations, community re-entry services and facility management. GEO doesn't just provide a job, GEO provides employees with a career they can feel good about. We adhere to the highest standards of quality and hire only those who strive to be their best." See "Careers," GEO Group, Inc., https://www.geogroup.com/Careers.

19. There are many analyses of the US immigration detention system estimating the financial cost, community impact, and size of the detention system itself. The numbers are overwhelming and concerning. "The immigration detention system has grown exponentially over the past 20 years from fewer than 7,500 beds in 1995 to the 34,000 beds mandated by federal law today [2015]. These beds are spread across a network of more than 250 detention facilities nationwide, including facilities run by for-profit corporations. DHS's Immigration and Customs Enforcement, or ICE, owns only 11 percent of the beds; 18 percent are housed in for-profit prisons under contract with ICE, and 24 percent are located in facilities owned by state and local governments that exclusively house immigrants for ICE. The rest of the beds are in facilities that also detain people awaiting trial or people serving criminal sentences." See Sharita Gruberg, "How For-Profit Companies Are Driving Immigration Detention Policies," Center for American Progress, December 18, 2015, https:// www.americanprogress.org/issues/immigration/reports/2015/12/18/12776 9/how-for-profit-companies-are-driving-immigration-detention-policies/.

20. The question of wages for detainees employed in detention centers is being litigated in US courts. "Forced labor is constitutional so long as it is a condition of punishment, a carve-out in the slavery prohibitions of the 13th Amendment. But in 1896, the Supreme Court held that 'the order of deportation is not a punishment for crime.' Thus, while private prisons may require work to 'punish' or 'correct' criminal inmates, judges in three cases have ruled that 'immigration detention facilities may not.'" What has not been settled is paying detainees a dollar a day for their labor. See Jacqueline Stevens, "When Migrants Are Treated like Slaves," *New York Times*, April 4,

2018, https://www.nytimes.com/2018/04/04/opinion/migrants-detention
-forced-labor.html.

21. Mejia, "Here, It's All Concrete."

22. Mejia, "Here, It's All Concrete."

23. Mejia, "Here, It's All Concrete."

24. In detention, as in prison, individuals are given a number, and this number becomes their identity within the system. The numbers detainees wear on their ID bracelets are called "a" numbers, where the "a" stands for "alien."

25. See Gregory Korte and Alan Gomez, "Trump Ramps Up Rhetoric on Undocumented Immigrants: 'These Aren't People. These Are Animals,'" *USA Today*, May 16, 2018, https://www.usatoday.com/story/news/politics/2018/05/16/trump-immigrants-animals-mexico-democrats-sanctuary-cities/617252002/; and Josh Dawsey, "Trump Derides Protections for Immigrants from 'Shithole' Countries," *Washington Post*, January 12, 2018, https://www.washingtonpost.com/politics/trump-attacks-protections-for-immigrants-from-shithole-countries-in-oval-office-meeting/2018/01/11/bfc0725c-f711-11e7-91af-31ac729add94_story.html?noredirect=on&utm_term=.336cba63fe77.

26. See, e.g., Beverly Roberts Gaventa, "Mother's Milk and Ministry in 1 Corinthians 3," in *Theology and Ethics in Paul and His Interpreters: Essays in Honor of Victor Paul Furnish*, ed. Eugene Boring (Nashville: Abingdon, 1996), 103–13.

27. Others have also characterized Paul as a border-crossing figure. Timothy Luckritz Marquis writes the following in the introduction to his *Transient Apostle: Paul, Travel, and the Rhetoric of Empire* (New Haven: Yale University Press, 2013): "The Apostle Paul has been known for centuries as a figure who transgressed and even straddled boundaries" (3; see also p. 12).

28. This is Christian tradition as recorded in the second-century writing *Acts of Paul and Thecla*, chaps. 3–4.

29. *Acts of Paul and Thecla*, chaps. 4–5.

30. "Most Americans do not think undocumented immigrants take jobs U.S. citizens want or are more likely to commit serious crimes. Most Americans continue to express positive views of undocumented immigrants when it comes to their impact on jobs and crime in the United States. About seven-in-ten Americans (71%) say that undocumented immigrants living in the United States mostly fill jobs that American citizens do not want. Nearly as many (65%) say undocumented immigrants are not more likely than U.S. citizens to commit serious crimes." "Shifting Public Views on Legal Immigration into the U.S.," Pew Research Center, June 28, 2018, http://www.people-press.org/2018/06/28/shifting-public-views-on-legal-immigration-into-the-u-s/.

See Brennan Hoban, "Do Immigrants 'Steal' Jobs from American Workers?," Brookings Now, August 24, 2017, https://www.brookings.edu/blog/brookings-now/2017/08/24/do-immigrants-steal-jobs-from-american-workers/. See also Josh Boak, "AP Fact Check: Trump Plays on Immigration Myths," PBS News Hour, February 8, 2019, https://www.pbs.org/newshour/politics/ap-fact-check-trump-plays-on-immigration-myths. See also the Pew

Research Center's "Immigrants' Contributions to Job Creation," October 22, 2015, https://www.pewsocialtrends.org/2015/10/22/immigrants-contributions -to-job-creation/.

31. I follow Angela Standhartinger's argument against Paul having Roman citizenship as Acts portrays. She writes that "in the first century, Roman citizenship was quite rare in the provinces, especially among Jews. Even municipal elites who were heavily involved in the imperial cult did not usually have it. Freedpersons in Rome and veterans received, if anything, Italian but not Roman citizenship." See A. Standhartinger, "Letter from Prison as Hidden Transcript: What It Tells Us about the People at Philippi," in *The People beside Paul: The Philippian Assembly and History from Below*, ed. J. Marchal, Early Christianity and Its Literature 17 (Atlanta: SBL Press, 2015), 109n7. In the same volume, Peter Oakes describes the Philippian community as being two-thirds Greek and about one-third Roman. He writes, "As well as being excluded from most land ownership around the town, Greeks were excluded from citizenship." He also concedes that, of all the Pauline communities, the Christians in Philippi had "possibly a higher proportion of Roman citizens . . . than in any other Pauline assembly." See Oakes, "The Economic Situation of the Philippian Christians," in Marchal, *The People beside Paul*, 70, 72.

32. Much of the discussion regarding Paul's Roman citizenship comes down to how historically reliable one takes Acts to be as a source, and where one places Paul in the social hierarchy of the empire. "Roman citizenship and citizenship in other cities of the empire was reserved for free men and entailed privileges only for the few. Citizens were exempt from being flogged, paid no tax, and were not subject to capital punishment such as crucifixion" (Elsa Tamez, "Philippians," in *Philippians, Colossians, Philemon*, ed. Mary Ann Beavis, Wisdom Commentary 51 [Collegeville, MN: Liturgical Press, 2017], 67).

For arguments against Paul having Roman citizenship, see, e.g., Helmut Koester's *Introduction to the New Testament*, 2nd ed. (New York: de Gruyter, 2000), 107. And, in more recent introductions to the Pauline letters, see, e.g., Morna Hooker, "The Letter to the Philippians," in *The New Interpreter's Bible*, ed. Leander E. Keck (Nashville: Abingdon, 2000), 11:467–550; and Daniel J. Scholz, *The Pauline Letters: Introducing the New Testament* (Winona, MN: Anselm Academic, 2010), 36.

33. Acts uses the detail of Paul's citizenship as a narrative trump card so that Paul, in the Acts narrative, can appeal to the emperor and travel from Jerusalem to Rome (Acts 25:10–11). Paul's appeal in Acts allows him to fulfill Luke's narrative trajectory: that Paul carries the gospel from Rome to the ends of the earth (see Rom. 15:20–24).

34. English translations warn Philippians to "live your life in a manner worthy of the gospel of Christ" in Phil. 1:27. But the Greek verb πολιτεύεσθε ("live your life in a worthy manner") comes from the same root as the Greek noun τὸ πολίτευμα, translated as "citizenship" in Phil. 3:20 ("our citizenship is

in heaven"). A better translation of 1:27 is "be worthy citizens of the gospel of Christ." See Julia Lambert Fogg, "Philippians," in *Fortress Commentary on the Bible: The New Testament*, ed. M. Aymer, C. Kittredge, and D. Sánchez (Minneapolis: Fortress, 2014), 548.

35. Christian tradition asserts that Paul was beheaded in Rome under Emperor Nero. Various Christian writings from the late first through the third centuries are used to establish this tradition (e.g., *1 Clement* 5:4–6:1).

36. See Elsa Tamez's commentary on Philippians and her discussion of the charges against Paul deduced from how he described his prison experiences ("Philippians," 13). See also Richard Cassidy, *Paul in Chains: Roman Imprisonment and the Letters of Paul* (New York: Crossroad, 2001).

37. See especially Standhartinger, "Letter from Prison as Hidden Transcript."

38. Tamez, "Philippians," 12–13.

39. Standhartinger argues that Paul most likely experienced torture in prison, because "in ancient legal custom, torture was part of a court proceeding; there was no way of gathering evidence, so an attempt was made to force a confession" ("Letter from Prison as Hidden Transcript," 121).

40. Tamez, "Philippians," 13–14.

41. Mejia, "Here, It's All Concrete."

42. Mejia, "Here, It's All Concrete."

43. Standhartinger considers that this danger deeply affects Paul's rhetorical strategy in writing to the Philippians ("Letter from Prison as Hidden Transcript," esp. 112–13).

44. See https://www.centrolegal.org/judge-orders-hugo-mejia-release -on-bond/.

45. Fogg, "Philippians," 553.

46. The Freedom for Immigrants storytelling project can be found here: https://www.freedomforimmigrants.org/storytelling-projects/.

47. For an alternative view, see Bryan Caplan and Zach Weinersmith, *Open Borders: The Science and Ethics of Immigration* (New York: First Second, 2019).

48. There are other crimes that lack a statute of limitations: murder, arson, and kidnapping. It is worth considering that in California there is a ten-year limit on the prosecution of rape but no limitation on the prosecution of illegal border crossing.

49. I volunteer with Detention Witness through Clergy and Laity United for Economic Justice in Ventura County (CLUE-VC), https://www.cluevc .org/immigrant-rights-2/immigrant-detention-witness/. See also "Visit," Detention Watch Network, https://www.detentionwatchnetwork.org/take -action/visit; Freedom for Immigrants, https://www.freedomforimmigrants .org/visitor-volunteer-resources/; and "Guide to Requesting a Visit or Tour of ICE Detention Facilities," Women's Refugee Commission, 2015, https://ccij .sfbar.org/wp-content/uploads/2018/04/Guide-to-Visiting-ICE-Detention -Facilities.pdf.

50. Fogg, "Philippians," 545.

51. Freedom for Immigrants is a national organization that can be found online at https://www.freedomforimmigrants.org/. Al Otro Lado is another organization located in California, but with opportunities for people to help from across the nation: https://alotrolado.org/. Matthew 25 / Mateo 25 is an organization in Southern California: https://www.matthew25socal.org/. The Young Center for Immigrant Children's Rights offers a newsletter at https://www.theyoungcenter.org/.

52. "We are focusing on these three groups of people who are especially at risk right now: undocumented immigrants threatened with mass deportation, as well as refugees who are being banned despite rigorous vetting; African Americans and other people of color threatened by racial policing; and Muslims, threatened with banning, monitoring, and even registration." See "What We Do," Matthew 25 SoCal, https://www.matthew25socal.org/whatwedo/.

53. See "Volunteer," Young Center for Immigrant Children's Rights, https://www.theyoungcenter.org/volunteer-at-the-young-center/.

54. M. Daniel Carroll R., *Christians at the Border: Immigration, the Church, and the Bible*, 2nd ed. (Grand Rapids: Brazos, 2013); Deirdre Cornell, *Jesus Was a Migrant* (Maryknoll, NY: Orbis Books, 2014); Ched Myers and Matthew Colwell, *My God Is Undocumented: Biblical Faith and Immigrant Justice* (Maryknoll, NY: Orbis Books, 2015); James Hoffmeier, *The Immigration Crisis: Immigrants, Aliens, and the Bible* (Wheaton: Crossway, 2009); Matthew Soerens and Jenny Yang, *Welcoming the Stranger: Justice, Compassion, and Truth in the Immigration Debate*, rev. ed. (Downers Grove, IL: InterVarsity, 2018); Miguel De La Torre, *Trails of Hope and Terror: Testimonies on Immigration* (Maryknoll, NY: Orbis Books, 2009); Jean-Pierre Ruiz, *Readings from the Edge: The Bible and People on the Move* (Maryknoll, NY: Orbis Books, 2011). See also the suggested readings in "For Further Reading."

55. Fogg, "Philippians," 543–56.

Chapter 6 Seeking Asylum at the US Border

1. "Adelanto ICE Processing Center was purchased by The GEO Group, Inc. (GEO) in June 2010 from the City of Adelanto. On May 27, 2011, GEO entered into contract with U.S. Immigration & Customs Enforcement (ICE), through an intergovernmental service agreement with the City of Adelanto." "Adelanto ICE Processing Center," The GEO Group, Inc., https://www.geogroup.com/FacilityDetail/FacilityID/24.

2. See John Moore, "An Immigrant's Dream Detained," *Lens* (blog), *New York Times*, November 25, 2013, https://lens.blogs.nytimes.com/2013/11/25/an-immigrants-dream-detained/?_php=true&_type=blogs&_r=0. For more recent statistics and an interactive map, see "Detention by the Numbers," Freedom for Immigrants, https://www.freedomforimmigrants.org/detention-statistics. Vice news service entered the El Paso detention center in 2019; see Evan McMorris-Santoro, Jesse Seidman, and Roberto Daza, "We Got Cameras inside One of the Biggest ICE Detention Centers. This Is What We Saw," Vice

News, August 2, 2019, https://news.vice.com/en_us/article/xweqgn/we-got
-cameras-inside-one-of-the-biggest-ice-detention-centers-this-is-what-we-saw.

3. See Cornell Law School, "8 U.S. Code § 1325.Improper Entry by Alien,"
Legal Information Institute, https://www.law.cornell.edu/uscode/text/8/1325#a.

4. Another misperception we have is that "fewer than half of Americans
know that most immigrants in the U.S. are here legally. In 2015, the most recent year for which data are available, lawful immigrants accounted for about
three-quarters of the foreign-born population in the United States. Just 45%
of Americans say that most immigrants living in the U.S. are here legally;
35% say most immigrants are in the country illegally, while 6% volunteer that
about half are here legally and half illegally and 13% say they don't know."
"Shifting Public Views on Legal Immigration into the U.S.," Pew Research
Center, June 28, 2018, http://www.people-press.org/2018/06/28/shifting-pu
blic-views-on-legal-immigration-into-the-u-s/.

5. See "Directory of Visa Categories," Travel.State.Gov, https://travel
.state.gov/content/travel/en/us-visas/visa-information-resources/all-visa
-categories.html.

6. For the history, financial costs, changes, and conditions of detention,
see "United States Immigration Detention Profile," Global Detention Project, May 2016, https://www.globaldetentionproject.org/countries/americas
/united-states#_ftnref2.

7. The National Immigrant Justice Center has analyzed data on detention
centers provided by ICE. They note that most detention centers are governed
by three distinct sets of standards, but that about 14 percent of detainees
(some 5,000 people) are detained in centers contracted under other standards,
including American Correctional Association accreditation guidelines. See Tara
Tidwell Cullen, "ICE Released Its Most Comprehensive Immigration Detention
Data Yet. It's Alarming," March 13, 2018, https://immigrantjustice.org/staff
/blog/ice-released-its-most-comprehensive-immigration-detention-data-yet.

8. See "Immigrant Detention Witness," CLUE-VC, http://www.cluevc.org
/immigrant-rights-2/immigrant-detention-witness/.

9. "Freedom for Immigrants is devoted to abolishing immigration detention, while ending the isolation of people currently suffering in this profit-
driven system. We are the only nonprofit in the country monitoring the
human rights abuses faced by immigrants detained by ICE through a national
hotline and network of volunteer detention visitors, while also modeling a
community-based alternative to detention that welcomes immigrants into the
social fabric of the United States. Through these windows into the system, we
gather data and stories to combat injustice at the individual level and push
systemic change." "Our Mission," Freedom for Immigrants, https://www
.freedomforimmigrants.org/our-values.

10. Sharita Gruberg, "How For-Profit Companies Are Driving Immigration
Detention Policies," Center for American Progress, December 18, 2015, https://
www.americanprogress.org/issues/immigration/reports/2015/12/18/127769
/how-for-profit-companies-are-driving-immigration-detention-policies/.

11. For example, "USA: Open Letter to Department of Homeland Security on US Asylum Report," October 19, 2018, https://www.amnesty.org /en/documents/amr51/9280/2018/en/; and Paloma Esquivel, "'We Don't Feel OK Here': Detainee Deaths, Suicide Attempts and Hunger Strikes Plague California Immigration Facility," August 8, 2017, http://www.latimes.com /local/lanow/la-me-ln-adelanto-detention-20170808-story.html.

12. See Fogg, "Philippians," 548–50.

13. I make the argument that members of the community of Christ embody Christ to the community in Fogg, "Philippians," 550–54.

14. Standhartinger writes, "When Paul, in the prescript to Philippians, does not call himself 'apostle,' but speaks of himself and Timothy as 'slaves of Christ' (Phil 1:1), we can read this as a description of the situation, for 'slave of Christ' not only includes a dutiful relationship toward the community or God (2 Cor 4:5; Rom 1:1), but also connotes a lack of freedom, distress, fear, and persecution (2 Cor 4:7–12), as well as human contempt (Gal 1:12). The self-description 'slave' matches the life experiences of prisoners and not only in antiquity." "Letter from Prison as Hidden Transcript," 114.

Chapter 7 Standing before ICE

1. The "Application for a Stay of Deportation or Removal" document is available to the public: https://www.ice.gov/sites/default/files/documents /Document/2017/ice_form_i_246.pdf.

2. A stay of deportation granted *to those without any criminal record* reflects the priorities of Homeland Security to deport illegal residents who have committed crimes. According to the US Immigration and Customs Enforcement Fiscal Year 2018 report, "ICE remains committed to directing its enforcement resources to those aliens posing the greatest risk to the safety and security of the United States. By far, the largest percentage of aliens arrested by ICE are convicted criminals (66 percent), followed by immigration violators with pending criminal charges at the time of their arrest (21 percent)." "Fiscal Year 2018 ICE Enforcement and Removal Operations Report," U.S. Immigration and Customs Enforcement, p. 2, https://www.ice.gov/doclib /about/offices/ero/pdf/eroFY2018Report.pdf.

3. On my college campus, for example, international students are here on one of three kinds of student visas, each with very specific terms for application and renewal and with restrictions on their travel and work. In addition to student visas, there are various kinds of residential status and worker visas—similar to student status, each has its own terms for application, travel, income, background, country of origin, renewal, and appeals.

4. According to the government web page, "ICE removes aliens from the U.S. who are subject to a final order of removal issued by an immigration court or following an administrative removability review. ERO [Enforcement and Removal Operations] facilitates the processing of illegal aliens through the immigration court system and coordinates their departure from the U.S.

ERO's robust removal program reduces the number of illegal alien absconders in the U.S. Removal management involves planning and coordinating removals across the country and developing and implementing strategies to support the return of all removable aliens to their country of origin." "Removal," U.S. Immigration and Customs Enforcement, August 2, 2019, https://www.ice.go v/removal#wcm-survey-target-id. See also https://www.ice.gov/.

5. Personal email, March 7, 2017.

6. To love of neighbors, Paul adds the love of those who are members of Christ's body (1 Cor. 13), and this love includes looking after each other's interests, which is to embody the mind, or character, of Christ (Phil. 2:4–5).

7. For example, Paul encourages the Philippians to share in each other's joy and suffering, as they share in Paul's joy and suffering (Phil. 1:29–30; 2:17–18). See chap. 6.

8. See Ben Daniel's discussion of Liliana's story and the implications for a second-wave sanctuary movement: "Liliana and the New Sanctuary Movement," in *Neighbor: Christian Encounters with "Illegal" Immigration* (Louisville: Westminster John Knox, 2010), 119–32. See also Andrea Castillo, "Churches Answer Call to Offer Immigrants Sanctuary in an Uneasy Mix of Politics and Compassion," *Los Angeles Times*, March 24, 2017, http://www .latimes.com/local/lanow/la-me-sanctuary-churches-20170301-story.html#.

9. The Sanctuary movement, renewed in the 1980s, "offers religious institutions and their members a chance to help those they feel deserve to stay. U.S. Immigration and Customs Enforcement has a longstanding policy of generally avoiding enforcement activities at 'sensitive locations' such as churches, hospitals and schools." Castillo, "Churches Answer Call."

10. Often used as a football term to indicate a last resort unlikely to succeed, the Hail Mary is a short Catholic prayer of intercession: "Hail Mary, full of grace, the Lord is with thee; blessed art thou amongst women, and blessed is the fruit of thy womb, Jesus. Holy Mary, Mother of God, pray for us sinners, now and at the hour of our death. Amen."

11. Vanessa Frank, the pastors' attorney and past chair of CLUE-VC, has graciously given her permission to include three of her emails written to the CLUE volunteers in March 2018. She hopes that by allowing herself and her commitment to advocate for immigrant rights to be named here, she has taken one more step on behalf of her clients to help people understand the real faces of the immigration crisis. Her work on behalf of immigrants seeking asylum, seeking to normalize their legal situation, and seeking advice on navigating the immigration process, is inspirational and unflagging.

12. See https://www.matthew25socal.org/.

13. See https://indivisible.org/.

Chapter 8 Where Do We Go from Here? Border Crossing as Praxis

1. I developed a curriculum for the Youth Ministry Network of the ELCA that may be a useful starting point for church groups, youth groups, or adult

Bible studies to begin thinking about boundaries and borders. This 2015 resource, "The Story of Scripture," includes my sixteen-page guide for group leaders, a PowerPoint presentation, an eight-minute video supplement, and a webinar. *Finding Jesus at the Border* further develops some of the themes introduced in this curriculum. The "Story of Scripture" materials can all be found online. Julia Lambert Fogg, "The Story of Scripture," for *Practice Discipleship 2015: Story*, organized by Colleen Windham Hughes, produced by the ELCA Youth Ministry Network, 2015, https://www.elcaymnet.org/PD2015.

2. Justo González calls this *el problema del ajo* ("the garlic problem"), which occurs when Christians from different cultural backgrounds try to share church resources. He discusses this cross-cultural problem in "Conflictos Culturales en la Iglesia Antigua," in *Para la Salud de Las Naciones: El Apocalipsis en Tiempos de Conflicto* (El Paso: Editorial Mundial Hispano, 2005), 66–78; available in English as *For the Healing of the Nations: The Book of Revelation in an Age of Cultural Conflict* (Maryknoll, NY: Orbis Books, 2002).

3. One of the more profound experiences my non-Muslim students reported when they took my "Introduction to Islam" course was their visit to the Islamic Center of Southern California. This mosque operates a food pantry in Koreatown, a vibrant neighborhood of Los Angeles, every Saturday. My college students could not believe the number of young Muslims from so many local and global backgrounds who committed their Saturday to feeding the people of Koreatown. They were grateful for how open, welcoming, and genuinely friendly the congregants of this mosque were to them personally when they arrived. See http://www.islamiccenter.com/food-pantry/.

4. Indeed, this is the entire mission principle behind Rick Steves's travel books, videos, and public-speaking events. Rick will take you to Europe and invite you to open yourself to wander and even get lost away from the tourist crowds to experience and discover something new in how other people live. What is wonderful about the United States of America is that we have so many microcommunities and minority cultures embedded in our towns and cities. You can travel outside your comfort zone simply by meeting your neighbors across town or at the other end of the state.

5. See "Alt.Latino," NPR Music, https://www.npr.org/sections/altlatino/; and, for immigrant voices, "Alt.Latino: Immigrant Songs," NPR Music, https://www.npr.org/templates/story/story.php?storyId=128247391.

6. See "Freedom for Immigrants," IMM Print, https://imm-print.com/author/freedom-for-immigrants/.

7. See "Undocumented Voices," Arizona State University Library, https://repository.asu.edu/collections/240.

8. See "Documenting the Undocumented: Immigrant Voices of Past and Present," UC Davis Library, https://www.library.ucdavis.edu/exhibit/documenting-the-undocumented/.

9. Some of these resources exist as oral histories in print form. See "Voices of Witness: Amplifying Unheard Voices," http://voiceofwitness.org/oral

-history-book-series/underground-america/. See also "Mapping Indigenous LA," https://mila.ss.ucla.edu/.

10. The Presbyterian Church USA position can be found here: http://oga.pcusa.org/section/mid-council-ministries/immigration/advocacy/. The Evangelical Lutheran Church in America social message on immigration can be found here: https://www.elca.org/Faith/Faith-and-Society/Social-Me ssages/Immigration. The United Methodist Church discusses its position on migration and immigrants here: http://www.umc.org/topics/topic-immigra tion. The Episcopal Church statement on immigration, migration, and refugees can be found here: https://www.episcopalchurch.org/OGR/migration -refugees-immigration. The United States Conference of Catholic Bishops' statements on immigration reform and advocacy can be found here: http://www .usccb.org/issues-and-action/human-life-and-dignity/immigration/church teachingonimmigrationreform.cfm. The Southern Baptist Convention's 2018 resolutions "On Immigration" can be found here: http://www.sbc.net/resolu tions/2288/on-immigration.

A coalition of evangelical leaders and congregations wrote an "Evangelical Statement of Principles for Immigration Reform" here: https://www.nae .net/evangelical-immigration-table/. And there are many more Christian statements of witness in support of immigration reform and of immigrant families in the US.

11. See also United We Dream (https://unitedwedream.org/), Make the Road New York / Se Hace Camino Nueva York (https://maketheroadny.org/), La Union del Pueblo Entero, or LUPE (https://lupenet.org/), and Mijente (https://mijente.net/).

12. See UndocuBlack Network, http://undocublack.org/.

13. See "The Network," UndocuBlack Network, https://undocublack .org/asdasd.

14. The "Family Unification Phone Project," CrowdRise, was created June 20, 2018, https://www.crowdrise.com/o/en/campaign/family-reunific ation-phone-project. Check organizations online for updated programs like crowdsourcing.

15. See Al Otro Lado, https://alotrolado.org/.

16. "We are a bi-national, direct legal services organization serving indigent deportees, migrants, and refugees in Tijuana, Mexico. The bulk of our services are immigration-related. However, the needs of the people we serve are diverse, so we also coordinate with attorneys and non-legal professionals in a range of areas such as family law, labor law, criminal law (particularly post-conviction relief), and employment law. We also assist families with aspects of reunification in Mexico when it has been determined by U.S. authorities that it is in the best interest of the child to live with his or her parent in Mexico. We work with non-custodial deported parents to ensure their rights as parents are protected in the United States family court system." "Who We Are," Al Otro Lado, https://alotrolado.org/who-we-are/.

17. See Pueblo Sin Fronteras, https://www.pueblosinfronteras.org/.

18. "About Us," Pueblo Sin Fronteras, https://www.pueblosinfronteras .org/index.html.

19. See Sanctuary Movement, https://www.sanctuarynotdeportation.org/; and John Washington, "Another Way to Keep Families Together: Join the New Sanctuary Movement," June 28, 2018, https://www.thenation.com/article /another-way-keep-families-together-join-new-sanctuary-movement/.

20. See New Sanctuary Coalition, https://www.newsanctuarynyc.org/.

21. See "New Sanctuary Needs You!," New Sanctuary Coalition, https:// www.newsanctuarynyc.org/all_training.

22. See "Get Support," New Sanctuary Coalition, https://www.newsan ctuarynyc.org/get-support.

23. See "Allies & Resources," New Sanctuary Coalition, https://www.new sanctuarynyc.org/allies-resources.

24. See "Habitat CEO: End Family Separation Policy at Border Immediately," Habitat for Humanity, June 19, 2018, https://www.habitat.org/news room/2018/habitat-ceo-end-family-separation-policy-border-immediately; Clergy and Laity United for Economic Justice (CLUE), https://www.clue justice.org/; "Catholic Charities Is Committed to Helping Immigrants and Refugees," Catholic Charities USA, https://www.catholiccharitiesusa.org /our-ministry/immigration-refugee-services/; "Protect Immigrant Rights," National Organization for Women, https://now.org/nap/immigrant-rights/; and "Know Your Rights: Immigrants' Rights," American Civil Liberties Union, https://www.aclu.org/know-your-rights/immigrants-rights/.

25. See "Support the Sanctuary Movement," Church World Service, https://cwsglobal.org/support-the-sanctuary-movement/.

26. See "Take Action," Church World Service, https://cwsglobal.org/get -involved/.

27. See Immigrant Defense Project, https://www.immigrantdefensepro ject.org/.

28. See Coalition for Humane Immigrant Rights, https://www.chirla.org/.

29. See "Migra Map," Migra Watch, https://migrawatch.wordpress.com /migra-map-uwd/. I accessed this site in April 2019, but be advised that real-time mapping and texting warning systems do (necessarily) move around online, so you may have to do multiple Internet searches to find them.

30. See "Mariposas Sin Fronteras Is Pausing Operations," Mariposas Sin Fronteras, June 2, 2019, https://mariposassinfronteras.org/.

31. See Immigrant Legal Resource Center, https://www.ilrc.org/.

About the Author

Rev. Julia Lambert Fogg, PhD, is Professor of Religion at California Lutheran University in Southern California, where she specializes in New Testament interpretation, first-century Christianities, and contemporary theologies from the margins. She also teaches for the TEEM (Theological Education for Emerging Ministries) program at Pacific Lutheran Theological Seminary. She was named Professor of the Year by the California Lutheran University class of 2008 and chaired the religion department from 2009 to 2016. She serves as chair of the faculty senate 2020–21 and as president of the Society of Biblical Literature, Pacific Coast Region, for 2019–20. Her teaching invites students to learn the historical background of scriptural texts in conversation with their engagement of local communities through experiential learning. Ordained in the Presbyterian Church, USA, and in shared communion with the Evangelical Lutheran Church of America, she has preached at and served Southern California congregations in English and Spanish. She serves in rotating worship leadership at the bilingual services for TheAbundantTable.org and writes for WorkingPreacher.org in Spanish.